CISTERCIAN FATHERS SERIES: NUMBER EIGHTEEN B

Amadeus of Lausanne

Eight Homilies on the Praises of Blessed Mary

CISTERCIAN FATHERS SERIES: NUMBER EIGHTEEN B

Eight Homilies on the Praises of Blessed Mary

by

Amadeus of Lausanne

Translated by Grace Perigo
Introduction by M. Chrysogonus Waddell OCSO

Cistercian Publications
Kalamazoo, Michigan – Spencer, Massachusetts

Amadeus of Lausanne
Cistercian Monk of Clairvaux
Bishop of Lausanne
c. 1119–1159

A translation of *Homiliae octo felicis memoriae Amedei episcopi Lausannensis de laudibus beatae Mariae* from the critical edition of G. Bavaud, *Amédée de Lausanne: Huit Homélies Mariales,* Sources chrétiennes, 72. Paris: Editions du Cerf, 1960.

Available from

Cistercian Publications
Studies and Texts in the Monastic Tradition

Cistercian Publications (Distribution)
Saint Joseph's Abbey
Spencer, MA 01562
www.spencerabbey.org/cistpub

Cistercian Publications (Editorial)
Institute of Cistercian Studies
Western Michigan University
Kalamazoo, MI 49008
http://www.wmich.edu/cistern

The work of Cistercian Publications
is made possible in part by support from Western Michigan University
to The Institute of Cistercian Studies

Printed and bound in the United States of America

TABLE OF CONTENTS

AMADEUS OF LAUSANNE AND HIS EIGHT HOMILIES ON THE PRAISES OF BLESSED MARY

THE LAST of Amadeus of Lausanne's eight homilies begins with a gentle complaint: 'Several days, beloved, have passed in which, under the burden of the episcopate and encumbered with great anxieties, I have been unable to provide your holy hunger the promised meal concerning the praise of blessed Mary.' Any conscientious bishop could, of course, refer in all honesty to the burden of his office and to his great anxieties, but Bishop Amadeus had better reasons to do so than have most. Amadeus had become bishop at a particularly tense period in the history of the vast diocese of Lausanne. Political difficulties and the irregularity of his personal life had forced the resignation of Amadeus' immediate predecessor, Guy de Maligny;[1] and Bishop Guy's fourteen years as Bishop of Lausanne, 1130–1144, had only served to exacerbate the chronic tensions between ecclesiastical authority and the wielders of secular power. Like Bishop Guy, Amadeus was to have an episcopacy of fourteen years, from 21 January 1145 (the date of his consecration—he had been elected earlier, in 1144) until his holy death on 27 August 1159. Unlike Bishop Guy, however, Amadeus brought to his high office all the qualifications of a saintly pastor of souls and of a capable administrator—qualifications which were to be tested to the utmost. As late as 1156 or thereabouts, Amadeus was forced

1. The definitive biographical study of Amadeus is by Father Anselme Dimier, *Amédeé de Lausanne. Disciple de saint Bernard*, Coll. Figures monastiques (Abbaye S. Wandrillee: Éditions de Fontenelle, 1949). Father Dimier provides the reader with virtually everything recoverable touching on the life and pastoral activity of our cistercian bishop. The biographical details of our own Introduction are based chiefly on material made accessible by Father Dimier.

to write his Easter Pastoral Letter[2] from a place of exile. The long-term open war being waged against him by his homonym, Amadeus de Genevois, had reached a particularly acute stage; and it was more than a bit ironic that the official charge of the rebel Amadeus was that of *advocatus* or *avoué* of the Church of Lausanne, the official whose responsibility it was to protect the temporal interests of his bishop.

Our homilies should be read against this background of violence and civil unrest simply because this was the *Sitz im Leben* in which they were composed, and because this somber real-life background brings out all the more the startlingly bright colors and radiant lights given off by these eight homilies. Page after page abounds in the luxuriant imagery of flowers, precious stones and gleaming jewels, gentle incense-laden breezes and fragrance of rare spices. True, the imagery becomes, at times, over-sumptuous; our senses become glutted. But even so, we ought to appreciate the springtime verdure because it contrasts so strikingly with the winter bleakness of Amadeus' usual landscape.

This is not to suggest that the concrete situation in which Amadeus carried out his difficult episcopal duties represents reality, and that the spiritual world depicted in such vibrant colors in the homilies represents an unreal world. Both worlds are real; or—better—both worlds form a single whole. But it remains true to say that the world of faith, so immediately present to the vision of the bishop of Lausanne, relativizes the all-importance most of us attach to the passing moment of our historically conditioned personal situation. Like each of us, Amadeus can experience to the full the impact of a given moment. There is nothing 'supra-temporal', for instance, in a letter he wrote from exile, in which he depicts an especially grisly scene: he has just finished celebrating Mass, and one of his followers is murdered even as Amadeus clasps him in a protective embrace; the episcopal vestments run red with the victim's blood.[3] But for all the immediacy of the present moment, Amadeus habitually remains conscious above all of the whole broad sweep of sacred history extending from the creation of all things to the final consummation of all things in the world to come; and it is this panoramic, totalizing vision which is responsible for the remarkable unity of the eight homilies *On the Praises of the*

2. PL 188:1299–1304.
3. *Ibid.*, col. 1299B.

Blessed Mary. But before we look a bit closer at these twelfth-century texts, a further word should be said about their rather impressive author.

THE *CURRICULUM VITAE* OF AMADEUS OF LAUSANNE

'God in whom we hope is present,' writes Amadeus in Homily III; and he adds one of the extremely rare autobiographical remarks to be found in these homilies: 'in him we have from our youth up been taught to trust' (p. 19).

Amadeus' religious formation began, in fact, well before the days of his youth. He was only a few years past the days of his babyhood when his father, Lord Amadeus d'Hauterives of the ancient and noble house of Clermont, turned apostle of monastic life and, sometime around 1119, brought to the newly founded cistercian abbey of Bonnevaux, near Vienne, not only himself but his ten-year old boy, Amadeus junior, and seventeen knight-companions as well.[4] Whatever else the senior Amadeus had given up in coming to the poor, struggling community of Bonnevaux, he had not given up the idea that his son should receive a solid education. At Bonnevaux the lad did begin receiving an education, but hardly of the sort deemed suitable by his concerned father. The philosophy of education held by the saintly Abbot John, the biographer somewhat sententiously tells us, was that 'the anointing of the Paraclete could teach the lad more in a second than the teachings of an apostate grammarian like Priscian in a stretch of many years'.[5] The force of the argument was lost on Amadeus senior. In a moment of depression he apostasized; and one day, probably in the year 1122, he took his son and rode off with him to the great abbey of Cluny, with its tradition of enlightened humanism. The account of Amadeus senior's brief, unhappy life as a monk of Cluny, his anguished repentance, and his return to Bonnevaux, belongs to another story. But if Bonnevaux could not provide Amadeus junior with a suitable education, neither could Cluny; for almost immediately the lad was sent for further studies to the court of his kinsman, Conrad

4. Details about the conversion of Amadeus senior may be found in the annotated edition of the *Vita Amedaei Altae Ripae* by Father Anselme Dimier, in *Studia Monastica* 5 (1963) 265–304.

5. *Ibid.*, p. 284.

of Hohenstaufen, the future Emperor Conrad Ill. The three years Amadeus spent in Germany could hardly have sufficed to complete the education of the adolescent, but we nevertheless find him in 1125, shortly after having fulfilled the minimum age-requirement for acceptance as a cistercian novice, knocking at the gate of Clairvaux. Clairvaux, of course, was the preferred monastic retreat for young aristocrats and university drop-outs.

At Clairvaux, the education begun spasmodically and continued at the court of Conrad reached its term. For fourteen years young Amadeus had the joy of living under the tutelage of Saint Bernard himself; and it was in this setting of Clairvaux, with all its contagious enthusiasm, *devotio iocunda*, and seriousness of purpose, that the stripling Amadeus grew to full manhood. The attainments of the mature Amadeus must have impressed even Saint Bernard, who, in 1139, deemed him ready to become abbot of the Savoyard abbey of Hautecombe. This monastery had been founded much earlier in the century, but had become affiliated with the Cistercian Order only in 1135. Amadeus' abbacy coincided with the change of location of the original abbey and the construction of the monastic buildings; and it was also under Amadeus that the consolidation of the cistercian ideals in the recently affiliated community took place.

The young abbot's gifts as administrator and spiritual father were considerable enough to draw attention to him well outside the immediate sphere of the cistercian family. For when the deplorable Guy de Maligny finally resigned his episcopal dignity in 1144, it was the thirty-four year old Abbot Amadeus of Hautecombe whom the clergy and faithful of Lausanne chose to succeed Bishop Guy. Accepting the burden of the episcopal office only at the insistence of Pope Lucius II, Bishop Amadeus remained very much Amadeus the monk. At no time during the troubled fourteen years of his episcopacy did the faithful of Lausanne find reason to regret their choice of pastor; and when Amadeus died on 27 August 1159, those who were with him were well aware that they were attending the death-bed of a saint. The liturgical memorial of Saint Amadeus of Lausanne is celebrated to this day, and is assigned in the cistercian calendar of saints to August 30.[6]

6. For complete details on the cultus of Amadeus prior to the calendar reforms of Vatican 11, see Dimier, *Amédée*, pp. 208–210.

THE HOMILIES

The literary remains of Amadeus of Lausanne are all but coterminous with the eight homilies *On the Praises of the Blessed Mary*. Apart from these, only two letters survive: the first to Count Humbert of Savoy (around 1148);[7] the second, the pastoral letter already mentioned earlier and addressed to the faithful of the diocese during the painful months of the bishop's enforced exile in or around 1156.[8] Also extant from the years of Amadeus' episcopacy are some fourteen official acts or fragments of acts;[9] and there is an outside chance that a page-long set of pastoral directives for confessors should be added to the list of Amadeus' writings.[10] But clearly, Amadeus' only serious claim to consideration as an author is his series of eight homilies devoted to the praises of Our Lady.

True, these homilies contain several allusions to their actually having been preached as a series of popular sermons in honor of the Mother of God—see, for instance, the exordium to Homily VIII. But medievalists caution us about taking such references too seriously. They are, we are often and rightly told, a literary device to be found in more than one sermon destined not to be preached aloud in church, but to be pondered over by the devout reader in the privacy of his room or cloister cranny. It would, of course, be unrealistic to envisage Amadeus declaiming these rather elegant latin texts before a cathedral congregation of people ignorant of Latin. But there is no need to propose the counter-hypothesis that the congregation was composed not of the people at large, but of the lettered cathedral clergy. After all, the polished latin text we have before us, if we care to look at the edition in the Abbé Migne's *Patrologia Latina*, Tome 188,[11] or—still better—the fine edition of the latin text established by Dom Jean Deshusses (a benedictine monk of the very abbey where Amadeus was once abbot) in Sources chrétiennes 72,[12] represents only one particular form of the text. We would hardly be wrong to presume a whole evolution in the history of the text as it passed through various stages from Amadeus'

7. *Ibid.*, p. 236.
8. Analyzed by Dimier, pp. 194–202.
9. Complete catalogue in Dimier, *Amédée*, pp. 236–239, with texts often given *in extenso* among the many documents included in the Appendix, pp. 257–416.
10. Dimier, *Amédée*, pp. 241–243.
11. PL 188:1303–1346.
12. *Amédée de Lausanne, Huit homélies mariales*, SCh 72 (Paris: Éditions du Cerf, 1960).

first rough notes scratched on wax-tablets to the final redaction in phrases of an elegant, sonorous (but somewhat limited) latinity. The existence of a latin text in no way excludes the possibility, or even near certainty, that these sermons were indeed delivered by Amadeus before an appreciative audience—but in the living language of his hearers, and in a version related to, but not necessarily identical with the polished latin text.

The printed history of these homilies is out of all proportion to the paucity of the manuscript evidence. Manuscript L 303 of the Canton Library of Fribourg (Switzerland) dates from the thirteenth century, and comes from the nearby cistercian abbey of Hauterive.[13] There is a second manuscript (without classification-number) from the Cathedral Chapter Library of Aosta, Italy; but this dates only from the fifteenth century.[14] Unimportant are the folios with a bit more than two of the homilies in the fifteenth-century Lausanne breviary manuscript, L 125 of the Canton Library, Fribourg.[15] The printed editions begin with the *editio princeps* printed at Basel in 1517, and prepared by the erudite Gervasus Sopherus. The text he followed was independent of the recoverable extant manuscripts; but since our humanist editor took the liberty of touching up Amadeus' Latin as often as it proved offensive to his delicate classical ear, this edition has to be used with caution; and since it was this edition which served as the basis of all subsequent editions, the same caution has to be repeated in every instance.[16] In practice, we would do well to ignore all the numerous editions prior to the *Sources chrétiennes* edition of 1960.[17]

Is Amadeus a good writer? Absolutely, so long as we refrain from comparing him with an absolute master such as Saint Bernard. Amadeus' sentences flow along in balanced periods; and he is particularly careful about the rhythm of the cadences. This makes for a pleasing musicality. Much less pleasing because of its cumulative effect is Amadeus' compulsive recourse to series based on the mystic number three. It is not enough for Amadeus to write at the beginning of

13. Description in SCh 72:46–47.

14. *Ibid.*, p. 47.

15. *Ibid.*, pp. 47–48.

16. Complete listing of printed editions in SCh 72:48–49; and Dimier, *Amédée*, pp. 235–236.

17. The history of translations is limited to french translations, and is given in the pages indicated in the preceding note; to this should be added, of course, the translation by Dom Antoine Dumas prepared for the Sources chrétiennes edition.

Homily I that 'this blessed Virgin [isl more brilliant than every light'; he instinctively re-enforces the statement by adding that she is 'more pleasing than every sweetness, more eminent than every dominion'. So long as this happens at the rate of no more than two or three times a page, the effect is not displeasing. When it happens more often, the reader begins to feel uncomfortable. But let the impatient reader take note! The theological content of the passage is usually rich in direct proportion to the multiplication of ternary groups. Thus, when Amadeus rings the changes on the Philippians hymn (Ph 2:9–10) in Homily VI, he is simply spinning out the pauline series: 'things in heaven, things on earth, things under the earth.' 'in truth,' writes Amadeus,

1.	the knee of those in HELL	bends before him in DREAD,
	the knee of those on EARTH	through SELF-INTEREST
	of those in HEAVEN	through their BLESSEDNESS.

2.	On the FIRST	he INFLICTS PUNISHMENT,
	the SECOND	he BRINGS OUT FROM THEIR WRETCHEDNESS,
	the THIRD	he RAISES IN GLORY.

3.	To the FIRST	he is TERRIBLE	in JUDGEMENT,
	to the SECOND	PITYING	in AIDING them,
	to the THIRD	GENEROUS	in REWARDING them.

4.	HE SUBDUES	the DEMONS	with his SWORD,
	REDEEMING	MEN	with his BLOOD,
	SATISFYING	the ANGELS	with the SIGHT OF HIS COUNTENANCE.

5.	Therefore HELL bends the knee,	TREMBLING at his POWER;
	EARTH bows the knee,	PRAISING his MERCY.
	HEAVEN bends the knee,	CRYING OUT: 'Holy, holy . . .'

The final member comes as a shock because the pattern is broken. Clearly, Amadeus should have written: 'Heaven bends the knee, crying out at his GLORY: "Holy, holy . . .".' A few lines later, Amadeus brings Mary into the pattern established by the pauline text, and shows how Christ has made her a sharer in his own lordship over heaven, earth, and hell:

1.	'He has brought to you	
	the SOVEREIGNTY OF HEAVEN	through his GLORY,

the KINGDOM OF THE WORLD	through his MERCY,
the SUBJECTION OF HELL	through his POWER.

2. All things with their diverse feelings respond to your great and unspeakable glory:

ANGELS	by	HONOR,
MEN	by	LOVE,
DEMONS	by	TERROR.

3. For you are

VENERATED	in	HEAVEN,
LOVED	in	the WORLD,
FEARED	in	HELL.'

Amadeus' thought seems to move in triplets. We might wish at times that he had been a bit more subtle, that he had given free reign less often to his obsession with ternary patterns. But we also have to admit that as often as not this ternary grouping corresponds to three objective stages or levels of reality, and that the literary threesomes correspond to a tripartite theological reality, or at least to a theological reality which admits to a tripartite analysis.

Apart from his concern for the rhythmic cursus of his cadences, and his ternary phrases. Amadeus' recourse to the tricks of the rhetorical trade are minimal. An occasional rhyme or assonance is probably simply fortuitous; and there is next to none of the wordplay so characteristic of writers such as Bernard. When we read in the Latin text of *Homily III*, for instance, that the incarnate Word 'implevit *sacratissimum et secretissimum sacra*mentum', we have before us an exception which proves the rule; so also in the phrase from *Homily VII*: 'Ibi *orienti* magis quam *morienti*, et *abiturae* plus quam *obiturae* . . . .' Whatever other difficulties of translation these homilies afford, Amadens has signally lightened the translator's task by avoiding the systematic use of assonance, consonance, rhyme, alliteration, and other forms of word-jugglery.

At the same time, Amadeus makes considerable demands on the reader, as do most of the really fine twelfth-century cistercian spiritual writers. They take for granted that the reader will be actively participating in the work at hand. The author has 'created' the text, so to speak; but it is up to the reader to accomplish the work of 'co-creation'. Amadeus gives us the image of a lily. He expects us to make that image our own; to be able to visualize what a lily looks like; to experience what its particular quiet splendor among flowers really is. He assumes that we know how to breathe in the fragrance of that lily, that we know how to admire its beauty. The problem with Amadeus, however, is that he keeps our spiritual senses and imaginative faculties working overtime. His pages teem with such a profusion of sights and sounds and fragrances and textures and tastes that there is danger of our becoming glutted by the superabundance of the fare—at least if we take seriously the work of 'co-creating' the text we are reading.

We moderns, truth to tell, are at rather a disadvantage compared with the readers of an earlier age. We are used to the realistic novel, to *verismo* opera, to the brutal explicitness of TV and the cinema. Everything is spelled out; our imagination is insulted; the work of conjuring up the images is done for us; and our interior senses are assaulted by the very violence of the medium to which we are exposed. In the case of mediaeval literature of the sort represented by these homilies, however, our role has got to be more active, more creative. We must learn, too, how to approach these texts in a frankly sensual manner; and our ability to do so is hard won these days. Most of us simply do not have the interior freedom requisite to make use of our senses in a fully human way; and this sort of freedom can be had only at the cost of a radical asceticism.

There is a difficulty on yet another score. The language of Amadeus is a symbolic language composed chiefly of biblical imagery (though more than one classical allusion or choice of words attests to Amadeus' exposure to the Latin classics). It is easier, certainly, to track down Amadeus' scriptural citations and allusions than is the case of Bernard of Clairvaux, since Amadeus is a bit more bald and explicit in the way he uses his borrowed language. Still, the basic difficulty caused by our relative unfamiliarity with the point of reference assumed by Amadeus remains. There is no question but that the biblical citations and allusions woven into our author's discourse contain clear ideas, precise concepts; but they also open out into other related directions. For all their precision, these biblical images and biblical statements function less as definitions setting precise limits to reality than as doors opening into deeper levels of understanding and experience.

We need not be too concerned over the fact, then, that we could be missing something by our inability to follow through with the rich implications of Amadeus' symbolic language. Missing something we certainly are; but what remains will be rich enough, for all that. Nor would Amadeus take it amiss if we occasionally read something into the text which he did not intend. This can be to our advantage, so long as what we read into the text harmonizes with the basic meaning of that text. Though the distinction would probably be lost on our author, he practises not only *exegesis* (reading *out of* the text) but *eisegesis* (reading *into the* text); and there is no reason why his readers should not do likewise. Amadeus was not interested in a text as an objective phenomenon existing in itself and independent of its readers or hearers. His concern was that the objective text be interiorized and rendered fruitful by those who make that text their own. Great care, then, should be taken at the level of explicit ideas and clear conceptual formulations; but to strip away the imagery and allusions and expressive overtones would be like analyzing the harmonic progressions of Bach's d minor *Chaconne*, and substituting this for the actual experience of playing or hearing the d minor *Chaconne*.

No one, absolutely no one, is going to catch all the allusions or spin out all the implications of Amadeus' language; and not many readers will be in a position to catch the monastic resonance and liturgical dimensions of Amadeus' citations. Take, for instance, the *exordium* to *Homily 11*, in which Amadeus exhorts us to hasten through the vivid brightness of Mary's paths 'with swelling heart and unspeakable joy' (p. 9). Do we recognize here a discreet allusion to the final lines of the Prologue to the *Holy Rule*, where Saint Benedict assures the tyro that, 'As we progress in our monastic life and in faith, *our hearts will be enlarged*, and *we shall run* with *unspeakable sweetness* of love in the way of God's commandments'. A quick check of the respective latin texts confirms the parallels: ' . . . *dilatato corde et inenarrabili percurramus laetitia*' (Amadeus); '*dilatato corde, inenarrabili dilectionis dulcedine curritur*' (Benedict). Moreover, the context of the two texts is rather similar: Mary grows in love as she pursues the path marked out for her in salvation history; the monk grows in love as he pursues the path marked out for him by God's commandments. If we now begin pondering the parallelism between the dynamic thrust of Mary's *curriculum vitae* and the dynamic thrust of the program for monks traced out by Saint Benedict in his *Holy Rule*, we shall probably be indulging in *eisegesis* rather than *exegesis*; but this is not to suggest that such *eisegesis* would be unprofitable for the reader. Relatively few readers could have been expected to catch on their own any parallel between the above quoted line of *Homily II* and the Prologue to the *Holy Rule*. Such readers will have missed out on an interesting thought worth their exploring in greater detail. But they have not missed out on everything, for they will still be able to grasp perfectly well the essential point Amadeus is making: Mary's life meant a constant growth in love.

Or again, take the mini-citation of Hebrews 7:4 in *Homily I*—six whole words: 'Behold how great is he.' The reader who enjoys verifying biblical quotations such as this one is bound to be a bit nonplussed upon finding that the author of Hebrews is here referring, not directly to Christ, but to his Old Testament prefigurement, Melchizedek. Is Amadeus handling his Scripture quotation with too light a hand? In point of fact, Amadeus is not quoting Scripture at all—at least, not directly. He is quoting a Night Office responsory: 'Behold, how great is he who comes forth to save the nations—*Intuemini quantus sit qui ingreditur ad salvandas gentes*.' This responsory was once in general use in the latin west in the Night Office for the Fourth Sunday of Advent. For Amadeus and his readers, the text would have carried with it a strong resonance of the final days of Advent when the birth of Christ, made present through the celebration of the liturgy, is almost upon us. The perceptive cistercian monk or nun would also recall that this same responsory did additional service in the Cistercian Night Office for the Feast of the Annunciation, 25 March. it is helpful to be aware of these resonances when we read the text of Amadeus' homily—helpful, but not per-essential; for what Amadeus has written makes glorious sense even if we fail to hear the expressive overtones, even if we do not feel ourselves bathed in the climate created by the liturgy of late Advent.

Amadeus' use of biblical texts can be particularly disconcerting with respect to his disturbing penchant for applying to Mary texts which are immediately applicable only to Christ. 'As death entered the world through a *woman*, so through a *woman* did life enter', we read in *Homily II*, where our author adapts Romans 5:12 to suit his marian context, and then straightway proceeds to do the same with 1 Corinthians 15:22: 'And as in *Eve* all died, so in *Mary* all rose again' (*ibid.*). We recognize, of course, the patristic theme of Mary as the New Eve, even while we regret that Amadeus touched on this classical parallel only by giving to the biblical texts a twist some of us might deem uncalled for. We are, after all, sensitive to the justifiable criticism of those theologians who rightly take exception to the kind of marian devotion which tends in any way to isolate Mother from Son. In this instance, Amadeus seems to be going a step farther by substituting the Mother for the Son.

The objection is a bit specious; and, if anything, Amadeus' tendency lies in the direction clean contrary to the objection that he disassociates Mother from Son. Central to our author's approach is the implicit conviction that christian existence means life in Christ, means sharing in Christ and his mysteries. Quite simply, Mary is the one who, in God's plan of salvation history, stands closest to Christ; she is the one who shares most perfectly in all the particular mysteries which make up the total Mystery of Christ. The stages of Mary's growth as treated of by Amadeus are so many stages in her participation in the Mystery of Christ. The pauline formula of life *in* Christ and life *with* Christ is predicable of any Christian who measures up to the exigencies of his or her vocation; but it is predicable of Mary to a supreme degree. Moreover, Mary's closeness to her Son means closeness to what Saint Augustine styled the 'Whole Christ', that is to say, Head and members, Christ and his Church. Here, however, the point is that the identification of Mary with Christ and the things of Christ is so absolute that, much to our discomfort, Amadeus can apply to Mary biblical texts which apply directly only to the Lord Jesus. Usually he is careful to add a saving qualifying expression. When he tells us in *Homily VII*, for instance, that the fulness of divinity remained in Mary bodily (a re-phrasing of Col 2:9) he is careful to add: *mediante Christo*—the fulness of divinity is within Mary bodily, because Christ, the incarnate Word, is within Mary bodily in the months preceding his birth at Bethlehem.

Perhaps Amadeus' understanding of the relationship between Mary and her Son, between Mary and the Church, can best be seen by a quick glance at the general thematic outline of our eight homilies:

MARY IN SALVATION HISTORY

Homily I	General Introduction: Mary between Two Testaments
Homily II	Introductory Schema of the stages of participation in salvation history, each stage of which forms the theme of one of the homilies to follow.
	Stage One (Homily II in strict sense) Justification of Mary; her embellishment with all the virtues in view of her unique vocation.
Homily III	*Stage Two*: Mary's nuptial union with the Holy Spirit; the virginal conception of Christ.

Homily IV	*Stage Three*: Mother of the Saviour; the virgin birth.
Homily V	*Stage Four*: The sword through Mary's heart; Mary and the redemption wrought by Christ.
Homily VI	*Stage Five*: The joy of Mary; Christ's Resurrection, Ascension, Glorification.
Homily VII	*Stage Six*: Mary's assumption into heaven; image of the future glory of the Church in heaven.
Homily VIII	*Stage Seven*: Final consummation or perfection; all Israel is saved.

The panorama is a vast one. Indeed, considering the fact that it begins with creation and the fall, and ends only with the final consummation of mankind in the world to come, it could hardly be more vast or more all-comprehending. Important for the matter at hand, then, is the fact that Amadeus views the Mother of God not only in the closest possible proximity to Christ and his Church, but views her against the whole sweep of salvation history. Further, all her titles to glory, all her prerogatives are displayed for us only in the context of Mary's place and role in the unfolding of the Mystery of Christ.

Amadeus' approach is essentially that of a theologian rather than that of an exegete—though we should feel a bit uncomfortable about pushing the distinction too far! Still, while the exegete begins with a biblical text and sees what ought to be drawn from it, the theologian tends to begin with the faith of the Church which he tries to understand and clarify by recourse to the inspired word and texts from tradition. The structure of Saint Bernard's homilies *In Praise of the Virgin Mother*[18] is provided by the lucan pericope upon which he is commenting; the structure of Saint Amadeus' homilies *On the Praises of the Blessed Mary* is a theological synthesis or outline which is the fruit of a theological reflection on the data of revelation handed down within the context of a living tradition.

Amadeus' claim to the title of theologian is a serious one. After all, he took a firm position concerning the *bodily* assumption of Our Lady and the clarity of his statement in *Homily VII* was such that two

18. *Homilies in Praise of the Blessed Virgin Mary*, translated by Marie-Bernard Saïd, OSB. Introduction by Chrysogonus Waddell, OCSO. CF 18A (Cistercian Publications, 1993). The two works were originally published as *Magnificat: Homilies in Praise of the Blessed Virgin Mary*. CF 18 (1979).

phrases from this homily enjoy the distinction of being cited in the 1950 papal definition of the Assumption, *Munificentissmius Deus*. He obviously enjoys it, too, when he can address himself to a theological query of the sort which provides material for several fine pages in Homily III, where Amadeus explains in what sense Christ can be said to come from each of the Persons of the Trinity. But the reader familiar with the patristic sources and biblical images he draws upon with such profusion cannot fail to be under the impression that Amadeus is essentially an eclectic thinker, drawing from many different sources, and not particularly concerned about tying up all loose ends. It is quite useless, then, to read into Amadeus anything smacking of the theologically subtle. For instance, when he refers to Mary as 'the tree planted in the midst of paradise' in Homily I, he touches on a theme of incomparable richness in the patristic and theological tradition of the Church; and it is precisely this image which features in what is surely the best available study of Saint Amadeus' Mariology—'Marie dans la Parole de Dieu selon S. Amédée de Lausanne,' by Dom André Louf.[19] But Amadeus' innovativeness in his use of a theme traditionally applied to the Church or to wisdom is probably as much the effect—–the happy effect—of his inadvertence as of his set purpose to use an ancient figure in an original way.

The theological approach of our author is reflected in what some historians of christian spirituality call his 'tender devotion'. In the Incarnation there is a meeting of the maximum of the divine and the maximum of the human. Not for a moment does Amadeus lose sight of either the human aspect or the divine aspect of this grandiose mystery, and the result is a deeply warm, even passionate, resonance which envelops the whole of our homilist's reflections on Mary and her Son. Possibly the supreme example of this is to be found in *Homily V*, devoted to the spiritual martyrdom of Mary at Calvary:

> Therefore, with deep calling to deep, two loves had come together into one and from the two loves was made a single love when the Virgin, mother gave to her Son the love she gave to God and showed her love for her Son in loving God. Therefore the more she loved, the more she grieved and the greatness of her love brought the increase of her suffering.[20]

19. *Collectanea OCR* 21 (1959) 29–62.
20. P. 45.

But Mary's sufferings were commensurate with the measureless love of the Mother not just for her dying Son, in whom she recognizes God crucified, but for her own people. Like any other christian writer of the period, Amadeus takes for granted a direct causal connection between what happened on Good Friday and the subsequent fall of Jerusalem and dispersal of the Chosen People in conditions of permanent pilgrimage and exile. Clichés abound; the invective against this 'criminal people' rises in rhetorical intensity. Canon G. Bavaud, who wrote the fine Introduction to the *Sources chrétiennes* edition of our homilies (latin text with french translation), mentions having once seen a passage from precisely this *Homily V* quoted in an antisemitic broadsheet.[21] The compiler of that broadsheet must have perforce been selective in what he quoted; for Amadeus insists that Mary's basic stance (and therefore the stance normative for the Christian) was one of unalterable love:

> Let no one argue that the Jews were hateful to the Mother of God for their having condemned her Son to a most shameful death. For those whom she saw near to eternal death she in no way considered to deserve her hatred and insult, but to deserve great affection, many tears, and a great pity. Therefore sharing in the charity as well as in the cross of Jesus, she took up her prayer for them . . . [22]

THE HOMILIES IN BRIEF

And now a brief note on each of our eight homilies.

Homily I introduces the series, and together with *Homily II* provides the reader with the hardest going. We begin with a heaven-ward gaze, 'examining the secret mysteries of heaven' (p. 1). The reader familiar with the classical latin liturgy will recognize, perhaps, a discreet allusion to the antiphon used for the Christmastide commemoration of Saint John the Evangelist in the ancient cistercian rite, *Iste est Ioannes*—'This is John, who reposed upon the breast of the Lord at the Supper: 0 blessed Apostle, to whom are revealed the secret things of heaven!' The reader, then, finds himself in the place of the same John to whom the Lord entrusted his own Mother, and who penetrated more deeply into the hidden realities of heaven, as tradition had it, than did all the

21. SCh 72:13.
22. P. 44.

other Evangelists. And 'first after the Redeemer' we see Mary, raised above all the angelic choirs. Who is this woman who is both virgin and mother? Only one person can really tell us: her own Son. This is a point of especial importance: Mary can be understood only with reference to her place and role in the Mystery of Christ.

The biblical text used as the organizing-text for this homily is a rather unlikely one: 'Support me with blossoms. Stay me with apples, for I am sick with love' (Sg 2:5). These blossoms or flowers are nothing other than the Old Testament adumbrations to individual mysteries which make up the total Mystery of Christ; and the 'apples' are the actual realization of all that had been foretold. This provides Amadeus with the elaborate picture he now paints, in which Mary is portrayed standing between two golden baskets filled with fruits and decked with flowers—the Old Testament and the New. And if the reader objects that he would prefer to see Mary, not between two baskets, but with her Child in her arms, that reader has missed the point. Mary is here placed at the meeting point between the two Testaments. She is at the very center where shadow becomes reality; and it is not enough for her simply to hold her Child in a mother's embrace: the fruit stands for the working out of all that makes up the total Mystery of Christ. So now Amadeus begins spelling out in detail the various stages in the unfolding of the panoramic plan for mankind's salvation—a plan in which Mary is beside her Son at every stage of its unfolding. The reader would be well-advised to go slowly at this point. Symbol is heaped upon symbol in luxuriant profusion, and the rapid scanning of a paragraph can result only in confusion for an impatient reader. The essential thread of Amadeus' argument is that the two Testaments are in accord. This he demonstrates by showing how: 1. the Old Testament *foretells* Christ and his Mother, and 2. the New Testament *reveals* Christ and his Mother. There is a final excursus in which Amadeus interprets the Holy of Holies and its furnishings in terms of Christological (and Marian) typology.

Homily II continues the preceding by adding to the portrait of Mary a detailed depiction of her splendid apparel and ornaments—images of the gifts and graces bestowed on her by reason of her high destiny as Mother of the incarnate Word. But Amadeus first states the general theme that Mary's life meant an uninterrupted progress and growth in love and virtue; and it is the stages in this spiritual journey which form the subject-matter of the homilies to follow. Amadeus summarizes the themes (already outlined above, pp. xviii–xix), and then relates each stage of Mary's progress with one of the gifts of the Holy Spirit. We can only be thankful that he contents himself with this, and stops short of relating the seven stages of Mary's progress to the seven petitions of the Lord's Prayer. . . . We now reach what, for the modern reader, is probably the most difficult part of the entire cycle of homilies: a detailed allegorical interpretation of everything that makes for Mary's beauty. Her apparel is analyzed on the score of its dazzling whiteness, its fragrance, its precious costliness, its variety (different colors, different purposes for each article of clothing). This is followed by a parallel allegorical interpretation of the various parts of Mary's body; after which Amadeus returns once again to each item of clothing in Mary's wardrobe. This homily is a gold mine for the specialist in mediaeval fashion-plates, but for most of us the text will be a bit difficult. Perhaps it might help to recall the tendency in times past to turn articles of clothing into allegories. Saint Paul did it with his bucklers and helmets and breastplates and shoes and the like; and until very recent times, the priest vested for Mass while praying brief formulas based on an allegorical interpretation of each article he was putting on. What marks Amadeus off as exceptional here is simply the ampleness and ruthless thoroughness of his allegorical analysis. But let us be careful not to lose sight of the spiritual realities which are, after all, the real object of our author's discourse.

Homily III deals with the incarnation and the virginal conception of our Lord. It begins with a moving prayer addressed to God the Father, whose love is so overwhelming that even omnipotent God cannot keep it within limits. All that follows, then, is a celebration of God's love.

The homily belongs to the type structured on a consideration of the *circumstances* surrounding the subject under discussion: who? why? how? for what purpose? Amadeus focuses his attention directly on the incarnate Word, and asks: 'Where have you come from?' The answer is: from the Trinity, from all three Persons. After a moving confession of man's impotence at discoursing on such deep realities, our theologian—and here Amadeus is obviously enjoying himself—explains briefly in what sense Christ comes not only from the Father and from the Holy Spirit, but from the Word. Next a splendid development based on the classical figures of the Incarnation: the rock, the fleece, the earth—all of which is a preparation for his presentation of the actual realization of the mystery heralded by the Old Testament types. The Virgin conceives the incarnate Word through the action of the Holy Spirit; and Amadeus reflects in glowing terms on the fullness of Mary's grace and on the action of both Holy Spirit and of Word within her. The homily ends in the best mediaeval tradition with an apostrophe addressed to Mary, in which Amadeus asks her what it must have been like to become Mother of the Word made flesh.

Homily IV, on the birth of Christ, is one of the longest of the eight homilies, and the least systematic as regards structure. The reader whose ear is attuned to classical literature will be startled and delighted to find Amadeus, in his *exordium*, describing the union of natures in Christ in terms borrowed from the legend of Orpheus and his lyre. Jesus is the new Orpheus; and it is to the music given off by the Sacred Humanity that we begin contemplating the virginal birth of the Lord. It was as virgin that Mary had conceived him, and it is as virgin that she now brings him forth. Mary is the New Eve; and Christ is the 'hand of God' (another favorite patristic image) which has brought life and healing and deliverance to countless numbers. Christ's birth, then, could only mean a perfecting, a consummating of Mary's virginity. The mystery is, of course, too much for us; and Amadeus, in a passage which deserves inclusion in any anthology of texts on faith and reason, asks us how we can expect to sound the depths of the mysteries of God when we cannot even fathom the mystery of a tiny mosquito. He insists, though, that 'he who does not know himself does not penetrate the deep things of God'. This entire passage is directed, it would seem, to Christians who exalt unreasonably the autonomy of reason (are there here overtones of the polemic crystallized in the affair of Master Peter Abelard?). But now Amadeus apostophizes two other categories of non-believers. There is an exhortation to the Jews not to refuse what Amadeus sees as the fulfillment of the Old Testament prophecies precisely through the virginal birth of the Messiah. This type of address is frequent in mediaeval literature. Much less frequent, however, is the last of these three exhortations, which is addressed to 'gentiles', that is to say, to Muslims; and it would seem that Amadeus is here borrowing freely from Peter the Venerable's tract *Adversus nefandam sectam Saracenorum*.[23] Just as Amadeus began his treatment of the virginal birth by referring to the Eve-Mary parallel, so also he returns to the same parallel to

23. PL 189:673–674.

close this section of the homily. He is now beyond polemics, and he breaks into a hymn about the joy of the universe at the birth of Christ; and when he begins speaking about the mysteriousness of the night of the Saviour's birth, his Latin rises to heights of incomparable beauty. There is nothing finer even in Saint Bernard's Christmas sermons. Saint Francis at Greccio is anticipated in the warm tenderness of Amadeus' meditation on Mary's joy at the birth of her Son in whom the hopes and aspirations of all ages now meet. But there is no *Schwärmerei* in any of this, and the intensity of the human dimension is achieved-precisely because the divine is ever present.

> The Wisdom of the Father clung round her neck and in her arms rested the Power that moves all things. The little Jesus stood on his mother's lap and in her virgin bosom rested that rest of holy souls. Sometimes tilting his head while she held him with right hand or left, he bent his gentle gaze upon his mother, he whom angels longed to took upon, and called her mother with sweet murmur, he whom every spirit calls in time of need.[24]

With *Homily V* we are plunged into the Passion of the Lord. Amadeus begins with a distinction between two types of martyrdom: that of the body, that of the soul. The Old Testament offers a number of martyrs of the heart: Abraham with knife in hand to slay his only son; Moses more than ready to die if only his people can be spared; David praying that the angel's sword turned towards his people be turned rather against himself. But the martyrdom of Mary at the foot of the cross surpasses all possibility of human reckoning.

> She stood near the cross that she might see her Son's sweet head anointed with oil above his fellows, beaten with rods and crowned with thorns—heart-rending sight! She saw there was neither form nor beauty in him who was lovely with a beauty beyond the sons of men. She saw him who was high above all nations despised and of no reputation, the Holy of holies crucified with criminals and malefactors, the eyes of the lofty man brought low, the head of the sustainer of all things sagging to his shoulders, the radiant face of God wither away and the glory of his countenance hidden.[25]

This God, then, is a hidden God; and Amadeus the theologian now sums up briefly traditional patristic teaching (Augustine, Leo,

24. P. 36.
25. P. 41.

Gregory) on the weakness of God as the means of the defeat of Satan. This leads to the long lament over the Chosen People who remain unmoved before God crucified, even as the universe takes part in the cosmic demonstration of bitter grief. The rhetoric begins like that of the standard mediaeval passages and tracts *Contra Iudaeos*, but it ends on a quite different note: love. Mary's martyrdom is caused not only by reason of her love for Jesus, but also by reason of her love for her own people. The final word, the inalterable word, is love, not hate. The final pages of this deeply moving threnody on the death of Jesus are devoted to the compassion of Mary, to the *Mater dolorosa*, and to the example of Mary's constancy and courage.

With *Homily VI* we find ourselves at the paschal banquet over which Mary presides. This is a wedding banquet, and the bread is the bread of life; the wine, the wine of the resurrection. Milk, honey, fatted calf-images of light, holy mirth, and universal joy succeed in rapid succession as Amadeus attempts to capture the note of paschal joy. if the faithful at large experience joy at the victory of Christ, what is the joy experienced by his Mother? So closely identified with Jesus is Mary that his victory is her victory. At this point, however, the paschal experience concentrated in a special way in Christ the Victor and his Mother begins reaching out to embrace a new human race. Christ was the seed that fell into the earth and died that it might bear much fruit. 'He laid himself down at seed time that he might at the harvest gather the human race'. The images become gloriously confused, and the earth in which this divine seed took root becomes Mary's womb, but also the baptismal font of the Church. A startling allusion to a single word from the Song of Songs—*acervus*, 'heap'—begins a long development based on images from that same Song. Mary's womb is the womb from which Christ is born, and it is also the womb from which the Mystical Body of Christ is born. The lilies of the Song of Songs are so many words of Scripture in affirmation of the Bride's virginal purity and beauty; and somehow Mary and Church become fused. The breasts of the Bride-Church are the two Testaments, providing nourishment suited to the condition of each of the children of the Church. The lilies return in yet another passage, but this time they are the souls of the saints who surround Mary, and who owe their beauty and their flowering to the victory won by Christ. The image of flowering reminds us, at least implicitly, that 'all flesh is grass', doomed to wither away. So Amadeus develops the theme that Christ flowers, not like the grass but as the Word, as the eternal days of heaven. His triumph is eternal and universal; and this is a triumph in which his Mother shares. 'The winter is past, the rain has departed and gone, the flowers of spring have appeared on our earth.' The time of eternal springtide has radically begun with the resurrection, and we are all invited to share in this joy with Jesus and Mary. But if the flowers have appeared, it is also time for pruning, which means that the wicked and the worthless are separated from the blessed. The resurrection, then, means both joy and grief. joy for the good, grief for the wicked. But the homily ends on a note of pure joy as Mary contemplates and shares in the glory of her Son. The homily is kaleidoscopic, and the images succeed in a variety of patterns which simply cannot be sorted out according to any demonstrably logical order. We begin, after all, at a banquet, and the wine is more than heady. The spirit is one of a joy that goes beyond all telling; a spirit of play, a spirit of improvisation. So, in reading this homily, we would do well to read it in the spirit in which it has obviously been conceived and written down.

Homily VII, on Mary's death and assumption into heaven, begins with a question: Why did Mary not follow Jesus as soon as he ascended into heaven? Why the delay? It was for the sake of the Church, Amadeus explains. For the Apostles in the first instance (how much Mary had to tell them about her Son!); but also as a source of consolation for Christians at large. The Redeemer was now in heaven; but the Mother of the Redeemer was still there as a visible sign of the fulfillment of all that had been promised. Mary's role, then, is ecclesial. Amadeus has a further penetrating insight. He sees Mary's gifts of grace as something contagious. To be close to Mary means to catch something of her purity and faith and humility. This is why she had to remain here below for so long, so that those approaching her could be enkindled from the fire of the Word which filled her, and could breathe the fragrance of the grace of the resurrection which she exhaled. Touching briefly yet again on his preferred theme of Mary the New Eve, Amadeus explains how Mary's prolonged stay on earth, at the very heart of the Church, was a preparation for her glorious reign in heaven. There is a quite remarkable development of this theme, in which Mary is shown as anticipating, even here below, the life of the world to come. The profusion of flowers and scents from the Song of Songs are used to depict the graces which flow from the Virgin Mother to the Church; and from the Church flow to us the rivers of peace and overflowings of grace that have their source in heaven. There is a particularly lovely paragraph, too, on Mary, Queen of Peace; for legend had it that the peace inaugurated by the birth of Christ lasted till the death of Mary. All of which, says Amadeus, should answer the question, Why did Mary remain here below after the ascension of her Son? But he gives one further reason for this delay: Mary grows to a beautiful and fruitful old-age as an example and model of perseverance.

The time has come, then, for Mary to follow her Son into glory; and the several pages describing Mary's leave-taking and her Son's reception of her in heaven are as fervent and lyrical as one would expect from a writer such as Amadeus. Without insisting on it, he quite clearly opts for the theological position that Mary is now in heaven body and soul:

> There [in heaven], having taken again the substance of her flesh (for it is not lawful to believe that her body saw corruption) and clothed with a double robe, she looks upon God and man in his two natures with a gaze clearer than all others, inasmuch as it is more burning than all, with the eyes of her soul and body.[26]

But Mary continues in heaven the role she began here below in the very heart of the Church; and the homily ends with an assurance that Mary has not forgotten for what purpose she was made Mother of the Redeemer.

Homily VIII is something of a cosmic synthesis. It begins with Mary as the tree sprung from the root of Jesse, spreading its branches over the whole world, and rising so high as to penetrate heaven itself. The fruit of this tree provides nourishment and a perpetual feast for earth and heaven. Several pages are devoted to Amadeus' explicitation of his view that Mary's exaltation and triumph form the obverse side to Satan's fall and defeat. Mary has taken the high place in heaven left vacant by the fall of Lucifer. For all her high estate, however, the Mother of Christ remains very much with us here below. In a particularly penetrating insight, Amadeus gives the reason for Mary's continuing love and concern for us:

> The more she beholds from on high the heart of the mighty King the

26. P. 67.

> more profoundly she knows, by the grace of divine pity, how to pity the unhappy and to help the afflicted.[27]

This leads into a long, sustained meditation on Mary's mediation. She is the Star of the Sea—though here Amadeus seems to be quite independent of Saint Bernard's splendid development of this theme. She is not content with past triumphs over the enemy, but from heaven continues, at the side of her Son, the battle against sin and the Evil One. But Mary's concern extends to bodies as well as souls, and Amadeus makes explicit reference to miracles of healing wrought in places dedicated to the Mother of God. She is a never-failing source of help and comfort, and her love goes out to saint and sinner alike. The final paragraphs are devoted to the glorious denouement of the whole Mystery of Christ, when, at the Last Judgement, the full meaning of all that has taken place will be made manifest in resplendent light; and the final words of Amadeus are a prayer that we too may find a place in the lovely country of heaven, in the bright resting places of paradise, amid the sparkling fiery jewels of the heavenly Jerusalem.

Those who pray the Liturgy of the Hours according to the Roman Rite will have occasion most years to read, as the patristic reading appointed for 22 August, the Memorial of the Queenship of Mary, a lovely passage on Mary, queen of the world and of peace, excerpted from Amadeus' Homily VII. This passage reads well even when taken out of its proper context—a bit like a particularly lovely song excerpted from a Schumann song-cycle. But to appreciate this song to the full, you must hear it in its proper place, with all that comes before and follows: which is why it is a good thing that we now have available a translation of the complete homily-cycle by Amadeus.

Readers familiar with French will find especially helpful the introduction and notes to the Latin-French Sources chrétiennes edition.[28] Perhaps even more helpful, however, would be the issue of *Collectanea O.C.R.* 21 (1959), devoted almost in its entirety to articles written on the occasion of the eighth centenary of the death of Saint Amadeus.

Chrysogonus Waddell, OCSO

Gethsemani Abbey

27. P. 71.
28. Above, note 12.

HOMILY I

EVERY HOLY and reasonable soul,* examining the secret mysteries of heaven and marking out the rank of heavenly spirits, finds first after the Redeemer the woman blessed among women, full of grace,* the one who brought forth God yet did not lose the glory of her virginity. This blessed Virgin, more brilliant than every light, more pleasing than every sweetness, more eminent than every dominion, lights up the whole world and renewing all things by the pouring forth of her precious ointment* surpasses the ranks of cherubim and seraphim both in power and majesty. Therefore let the King, through her glorious merits, admit us to his chamber* and David's offspring, who shuts and no one opens,* will disclose to us his hidden secrets. He opens and no one shuts. Let him reveal to us the joys of her who bore him, the beauty of his chosen Mother.

*Cf. Rm 12:1

*Lk 1:28

*Is 39:2, cf. Am 6:6

*Sg 1:3, 2:4

*Rev 3:7 = Magnificat antiphon for 20 December

Moses and the prophets have borne witness to her. Evangelists and doctors later took up the story of her life, her habits and her grace, that the truth might be consistently related and that what the first had foretold should be the second might describe as having been accomplished. Therefore, inspired by so many illustrious persons, let us hasten towards that odor of her perfumes and draw towards us the breath of her graces. And while we are yet separated and held back from the delight of beholding her, let us rest among her flowers, on which in the Canticle she bids us be supported, saying: 'Support me with blossoms. Stay me with apples, for I am sick with love.'*

*Sg 2:5

What are these flowers if not the divine mysteries in praise of her and the sacred mysteries once hidden from the world* which, now appearing in the flesh and manifested in the spirit,* have come forth from the sayings of the Fathers like buds from the trees. The Apostle explains these 'apples' by saying: 'The fruits of the spirit are love, joy, peace, patience, goodness, kindness, longsuffering, gentleness, faith, modesty, temperance, chastity.'*

**Col 1:26*
**1 Tim 3:16*
**Gal 5:22-3*

She is supported with flowers when the oracles foretold are clear. She is stayed with apples when what was written comes to pass. 'Give her of the fruits of her hands and let her works praise her in the gates.'* But because the words treat of true flowers and the unfading fruit of justice, we must, aided by the gift of the Spirit, examine more closely those same flowers and fruits.

**Prov 31:31*

Let us notice therefore two golden baskets, as it were, filled with fruits and decked with flowers: the New Testament and the Old, standing on this side and on that, on the left hand and on the right of the Virgin. Of these the ancient one passes to the left and the new by grace shines on the right. For justly is the law of death on the left and the law of life on the right, for the former produces the sinner and the latter takes away sin. The Virgin of virgins herself is seen in springtime among the flowers and delighting in the sweetness of the fruits and, like the tree planted in the midst of paradise,* she raises her head to the height of heaven and, conceiving by the heavenly dew, brings forth the fruit of salvation, the fruit of glory, the fruit of life, and he who eats of it will live for ever.*

**Gen 2:9, 3:3*
**Gen 3:5, cf. Jn 6:59*

That what has been said may be clear, paradise is the garden to which the Church invites its beloved. 'Let my Beloved come into my garden and eat the fruit of her trees.'* She calls herself the garden of the beloved, she whom the Saviour's springs water,* the streams of his gifts inebriate, so that being wedded she rejoices in the love of the Spirit and, made fruitful by the drops of his dew,* she exults in the birth of many sons, as it were, in the profusion of

**Sg 5:1*
**Is 12:3*
**Ps 65:10*

her progeny. Here she calls the beloved to eat the fruits of the trees, for she keeps for him fruits new and old*, that is, the words of the two Testaments, or the perfect thoughts of her heart which serve for her breasts, as one reads: 'Thy breasts shall be as the grapes of the vine',* or surely all good spirits of angels and of men, some of whom persevere in newness of life, some grieve by reason of their age and of their sin.

*Sg 7:13
*Sg 7:8

By fruits new and old can also be meant the Fathers new and old, among whom is nourished love of the spouse until the day dawns and the shadows fade.* Among these and in their midst rises the tree which we have called the tree of salvation, bearing the food of life and the heavenly manna—manna possessing all delight and all sweetness,* and if the first Adam had touched it he would never have tasted death. This bread the Son of Man in the Gospel declares himself to be, saying: 'I am the living bread who came down from heaven. If any man eats of this bread, he will live for ever.'*

*Sg 2:17
*Ws 16:20
*Jn 6:51-2

Let us therefore return to the baskets mentioned before and let us consider the flowers on the left and the fruits on the right. For what the Law promised in the flowers, grace showed clearly in action, and there is foretold what is to be. Here is praised virtue brought to perfection. There is the sign, here the actuality of the sign. Let us see the same baskets representing the glory of Christ and the childbearing of the Virgin. For this is the completion, this is the end of the Testaments: to proclaim Christ, to show forth Christ, to announce Christ, and the Virgin Mary.

And that indeed is hidden under signs, now it is cloaked in mysteries and metaphors, now celebrated in festal rite, now disguised by sacrifices, now made clear in prophecy or confirmed by the declaration of the Gospel. And in this thicket of Lebanon*, on this thick shadowed mountain, there is revealed to us the worthiness of the Spouse and the couch from which he issues*, the Saviour of the world and the soil bringing forth the Saviour*, the star out of Jacob†, the leader from Israel, the rod from the stem of

*1 Kg 10:17
*Ps 19:5
*Is 45:8
†Num 24:17

**Is 11:1* Jesse, the flower from his root*. For in one place we
**Cf. Is 7:14* read that Christ shall be born of a virgin,* will suffer
in the flesh, will rise again in glory, will ascend in
**Ps 47:5* triumph,* will sit at the right hand of the Father and
will bestow the gifts of the Spirit upon believers. In
another place [we read] that he was born, suffered,
rose, ascended and pours the gift of the Spirit upon
his own.

Thus in the writings of truth it was announced of
holy Mary that a virgin should conceive and a virgin
**Is 7:14* should bring forth a son, his name Emmanuel,* His
going forth should be from the beginning, from the
**Micah 5:2* days of eternity.* Him the virgin was worthy to con-
ceive, she alone to bring forth, to suckle, amidst the
prayers and ardent expectations of the Church as it
prays and says: 'Who would give me you as my
brother, sucking my mother's breasts, that I may find
you without and kiss you and no one shall now
**Sg 8:1* despise me.'*

I shall find you, she says, without, in the light, you
who are the Father's secret. I shall find you appearing
in the flesh, who are hidden in invisible majesty. I
shall find you, the bridegroom, coming forth from
**Ps 19:5* the marriage chamber,* who was conceived in the
Virgin's womb by the Holy Spirit. And I shall kiss
you in the flesh you have assumed, which is united
to you. I shall kiss you, being joined to you in the
partaking of your flesh and blood, so that no longer
**Gen 2:24, 1 Cor 6:16* are we two but one flesh.* I shall kiss you, clinging
to you in one Spirit, for he who clings to God is one
**1 Cor 6:17* spirit [with him].* And now no one will despise me.
Not God the Father, seeing his own Son incarnate,
not a holy angel adoring God made man, not a proud
demon grieving that he has been defeated by Christ.

For the rest, let us bring in some points from the
Gospel. We read that the Virgin was saluted by the
angel, espoused by God, that she conceived by the
**Lk 1:26-38* Holy Spirit,* brought forth true God and true man,
**Mt 1:21* who should save his people from their sins,* and of
**Lk 1:33* whose kingdom there should be no end.* He it is who
was promised to Abraham, that in his seed all the
**Gen 22:18* nations should be blessed.* Of him the Apostle fitly

says: 'Behold how great is he'* who comes forth to save the nations. Truly great is he whom the Father sent into the world as his only begotten Son, whom the spiritual Virgin poured forth, whom a Virgin conceived and brought to birth, and after the birth remained a virgin.

*Heb 7:4

He is announced by the archangel, conceived by the Holy Spirit, and is revealed by John while he was still enclosed within his mother's womb.* He is taken up by the aged Simeon with joy unspeakable and by him is foretold as the light of the nations and the glory of the people Israel.*

*Lk 1:41

*Lk 2:28-32

Do you therefore see how wisdom reaches boldly from end to end and disposes all things pleasantly?* From a child as yet unborn to a feeble old man it proclaims such consistent evidence and with such sweet harmony of truth plays upon the instruments. Hence it is said by the prophet: 'There is no one who can hide from its heat.'* He came forth from the Father, he returned to the Father. He went into hell, he returned to the throne of God. Who would be hidden from the heat of him whom an infant in the womb perceived, and by whom a chilled old man in the temple was set on fire? As if to signify that he willed to meet the Lord, the one rejoiced in what movement he could make. Taking into his arms Jesus whom he was awaiting with unspeakable longing, the other received divine love into the centre of his being, and not able to endure in his frail flesh the sweet warmth of the being who is above the heavens or in his frame the power of the firebearing word, he prayed for the dissolution of his body, that when his mortal habitation was destroyed he might enjoy more freely the sweetness he already tasted and might announce to those dwelling in the shadow of death* the birth of the Saviour whom he was proclaiming among those on earth.

*Wis 8:1 = *Magnificat* antiphon for 17 December

*Ps 19:6

*Lk 1:79

But what are we doing or whither are we being carried? See, while we desire to extol her that was blessed among women,* we are praising the blessed fruit of her womb,* and while we seek to commend the beauty of the tree, we keep close to the

*Lk 1:28

*Cf. the 'Hail Mary'

surpassing beauty of the fruit. For every tree is known by its fruit and is judged by its own yield.* As the palm is assessed according to the sweetness of its dates, the olive tree by the richness of the olives, the wine by the juice of the grape, so the praise of the Son enriches the Mother and the divine birth heaps honor upon her that bore him.

**Cf. Lk 7:20*

It is pleasing, beloved, to repeat with another meaning what has already been set forth and to confirm it by a fresh statement, so that blind unbelief may be refused by the light, and faith in Christ reveal itself clearly and without hindrance.

Let us therefore enter the Holy of Holies and gaze upon the mercy seat, which has above it two cherubim gazing upon it and overshadowing it as they face each other with wings outstretched.* There among other things shines the golden urn enclosing hidden manna. There is Aaron's rod which budded.* Understand that this is the mercy seat of which the Apostle says that he is the propitiation for our sins.* The two cherubim mean the two Testaments, for 'cherubim' means the fulness of knowledge, and the fulness of knowledge is in the Testaments. Rightly do the cherubim cover the mercy seat which they gaze upon as they face each other, for they conceal under figures and riddles the Christ whom the Testaments agree in proclaiming.

**Cf. Ex 25:17-20*

**Heb 9:4*

**1 Jn 2:2*

The golden urn is blessed Mary, golden by reason of the excellence of her life, golden through her integrity and purity, golden through the fulness of grace. This urn held the hidden manna,* she who in her sacred womb bore the bread of angels which comes down from heaven* and gives life to the world.

**Cf. Rev 2:17*

**Cf. Jn 6:30, Ps 78:24*

Further, the priestly rod signifies that same glorious one who, descended from a priestly and royal stock, gave birth to the King of saints, who is a priest for ever after the order of Melchizedek.* Truly is she called a rod for she is gracious and upright, sensitive and straight. Gracious through her modesty and beauty, upright through her justice and rectitude, sensitive through her capacity for

**Ps 110:4, Heb 5:6,10 & 6:20*

contemplation, straight through the merit of her life. She blossomed by the power of the Holy Spirit as Aaron's rod [blossomed] by miracle.* That rod put forth the fruit of the almond, she gave forth the finest almond, that has kernel and shell: kernel to restore, shell to protect. Kernel in his divinity, shell in his humanity.

*Num 17:8

Do you wish to know the kernel? Hear that 'in the beginning was the Word'.* Do you desire to know the shell? Hear: 'The Word was made flesh and dwelt among us.'* You see therefore that the kernel in the shell is the Incarnate Word. And since the shell has a rind, interpret the shell as the bitter woe of the flesh, the shell as the resurrection, the kernel as the divinity. By the rind Christ heals us, but the shell strengthens us [and] by the kernel ministers to us eternal life.

*Jn 1:1

*Jn 1:14

Let this kernel, this Word, again and again shed light upon us and bring us to his mother's chamber.* He who lives and reigns with God the Father in the Unity of the Holy Spirit, God through all ages. Amen.

*Cf. Sg 3:4

HOMILY II

SINCE WE HAVE, at the bidding of God, embarked upon the praises of the Blessed Virgin, it remains for us to complete her praise from the bottom of our heart and with dutiful voice. Let us gaze upon her glory and, entering the depth of so great a light, let us with swelling heart and unspeakable joy hasten through the vivid brightness of the paths, saying with Solomon, 'Her paths are lovely and all her ways are peaceful'.* What if, as the same prophet says, 'the path of the just, as a shining light, goes forth and grows into the perfect day'?* Who will be able to express the light and brightness of her paths? Yet we shall try to explain in part the progress and additions of her paths so that she may be perceived as glorious in her steps and be proclaimed in each of them.

*Prov 3:17

*Prov 4:18

For she possessed progress clearly marked and distinct growth, so that she advanced according to the fairest order of charity and,* going forward from virtue to virtue, she saw the God of gods in Sion,* being changed from glory to glory as by the Spirit of the Lord.*

*Sg 2:4

*Ps 84:7

*2 Cor 3:18

Firstly, therefore, she was deemed worthy to be adorned with the beauty of all the virtues. Secondly she was united to the Holy Spirit in a bond of wedlock. Thirdly, she was found the Mother of the Saviour. Fourthly, a sword pierced her soul and by the flesh taken of her flesh the ruin of the lost world is restored. Fifthly, she rejoices in her Son arising and ascending above the heaven of heavens to the right hand of the Father. Sixthly, she is caught up from this world and as the Lord hastens to meet her she is placed above the denizens of heaven. Seventh, she will be completed when the fulness of the Gentiles shall have entered and all Israel shall be saved.* For beyond what it is right to be said or believed, she rejoices in the general salvation of the elect, knowing that it was for them that the Son of God took flesh from her. Therefore she will then be fulfilled, God providing a better thing, lest without us she should not be made perfect.*

*Rom 11:25-6

*Heb 11:40

But now let us consider the names of those steps. The first can be called justification or embellishment, the second union or alliance, the third the Virgin birth or new offspring, the fourth vigor of mind or martyrdom, the fifth joy or wonder, the sixth assumption or exaltation, the seventh fulness or perfection.

The aforesaid justification or embellishment proceeds from the fear of God. Union and alliance come forth from an amazing piety. For the virgin birth and the new offspring shed the light of knowledge upon the universe. The work of fortitude was revealed in the dying of Christ and his mother's watching it. But when he arose the deep and unfathomable plan by which he deceived the cunning foe and redeemed the world poured forth into joy and wonder. Then when the heavens are opened, invisible blessings are revealed, and something wonderous comes to pass, so that, as God in man learned by experience the sufferings of man, so man taken up into God learns with full understanding the glory of God. Finally wisdom will bring fulfilment and perfection so that she will appear perfect in the perfect and will exult in her fulfilment.

Let us repeat what has been said and, lingering again in those same steps, let us contemplate the Lord, clinging to the ladder, and the angels ascending and descending* towards the Virgin. For they marvel at the pure maiden, the mother of the Lord, soon to be the queen of heaven, and they break forth in these words of wonder and praise: 'Who is she who ascends in pure whiteness?'*

*Gen 28:12

*Sg 3:6

What is 'pure whiteness' if not adornment with white vesture? Adorned surely with the adornment of beauty and honor, of righteousness and holiness. The greatest of the prophets shone with the adornment of these garments when he said, 'I will rejoice greatly in the Lord and my soul will exult in my God, for he has clothed me with the garments of righteousness as a bridegroom adorned with a garland and as a bride with her jewels.'* Hence the psalmist says to God: 'Let your priests put on righteousness.'* But Isaiah exhorts Jerusalem to shake off the dust and be clothed with the garments of her glory.* And in reproach to the first angel it is said, 'You too have been a sign of the likeness in paradise of the delight of God. Every precious stone was your covering, sard, topaz, jasper, chrysolite, onyx, beryl, sapphire, carbuncle, and emerald.'* But we ought to know that these garments are white and fragrant, precious and diverse. White for innocence and purity and for the brightness of eternal light, fragrant for the perfume of esteem and good repute, precious because of their excellence and appropriateness, diverse because of their differing uses and varied shapes.

*Is 61:10
*Ps 132:9
*Is 52:2
*Ezk 28:12-13

Concerning the whiteness, it has already been said, 'Who is she who ascends in pure whiteness?'* And elsewhere we read, 'Who is she who goes forth as the rising dawn, beautiful as the moon, excellent as the sun?'* *As the dawn rising* from darkness to light, from error to faith, from the world to God, and in the faint gleam of her rising, tinged with the crimson of modesty, with the lovely pallor of humility. *Beautiful as the moon* because for ever remaining chaste, she is bathed in the brilliance of heavenly light and rejoices in its overshadowing. Everywhere brilliance, everywhere splendor, everywhere the whiteness of her garments is signified.

*Sg 3:6
*Sg 6:9

Of this whiteness other things might have been said, as that word of the Lord, who said concerning his own: 'They shall walk with me in white for they are worthy',* and 'He who has conquered shall be clothed in white garments'.* But we are hard pressed by our desire for brevity.

*Rev 3:4
*Rev 3:5

Now let us hear concerning the odor of the same
garments the words of the bridegroom praising the
bride in the marriage song: 'The odor of your
Sg 4:11 garments is as the odor of incense.'* They say that by
the odor of incense demons are put to flight, tears are
evoked, God is appeased by intercessory tears. I
would gladly have said that by the odor of Mary's
virtues the angels of darkness are put to flight and are
carried hither and thither by a kind of strong whirlwind, so that in them is fulfilled what was written,
Ps 35:5 'They became as the dust before the wind.'* That
odor awakens those dead in their sins, strengthens
feeble souls, urges on the good towards things better,
and the better to things that are best. A good odor,
which through the virgin called forth the king on his
couch, so that coming to us he might receive what is
ours, give us what is his, and establish, by unchanging
law and unending peace, friendship with us. Thus
therefore the fragrance of holy Mary's garments puts
enemies to flight, attracts the good and placates God.

Concerning their richness and variety, in speaking
to one lovely beyond the sons of men, the psalmist
sings in praise of the bride saying, 'The queen stood at
Ps 45:9 his right hand in vesture of God, clad in many hues,'*
and a little afterwards he added, 'All the glory of the
king's daughter is within, clothed with fringes of
Ps 45:14 gold.'* Not only is she adorned with vesture of gold
and golden fringes, but also with a covering which, as
Prov 31:22 Solomon says, she made for herself.*

Ezk 28:13 And she is covered with every precious stone.*
For no gem, no precious stone, no rich pearl is lacking from her covering, until no longer can it be called
[just] rich, but justly rich beyond all richness. For
just as one richness, spreading in a moment or rather
every moment of a moment and part of a moment
produces many riches, so many converge into one so
that they become one by sharing in one. And this
richness is charity, the bridal robe, the robe without
Eph 5:27 spot or wrinkle,* the robe that cannot be torn,
Jn 19:23 without seam, woven in one piece.* From this,
Rm 11:36 through this and in this* are all things dear, whatever
things are good. And they are all one in unity, the

same in identity, simple in simplicity. In the whole they hold the whole and in the whole they rejoice far removed from any lessening or increase, from any diversity or multiplicity.

We have spoken about the richness of the ornaments. Let us now discuss their variety, some examples of which we set forth above. Of this there are two kinds, one of color, the other of use.

This variety which exists in color is divided into white and black, red and green. These are said to be the primary colors and these in particular adorn the aforesaid garment. It is green as the olive or laurel and as the rainbow showing green in the clouds. It is green in the faith and hope of the eternal, in obedience to the commandments, in the contemplation of eternal greenness and the greenness of eternity. It is red like a fiery globe, as a king's purple,* as a twice-dyed scarlet* cloth betokening the love of God and of one's neighbor. Its black is like horn and like buds of palm trees, or else surely like painted ivory and like a still heaven at midnight. That color is set as the foundation and it underlies the other colors so that it signifies to us that the virtue of humility should be laid down as a foundation. If we seek for whiteness, it shines by means of perpetual virginity and perfect purity. Also by the charm of its beauty it turns back the mighty rhinoceros and attracts the God of majesty. Many other things of spiritual meaning can be found by the spiritual on the subject of the variety and meaning of the colors.

*Sg 7:5
*Ex 25:4

But variety which suitably serves for use shines forth also in many ways. For some ornaments cover and adorn the lofty head and neck of the blessed one, some her hair and ears, some her breast and arms, some her hands and fingers. Some of them clothe her whole body, some encircle her thighs, some protect her feet.

Her head signifies her mind. For just as the head controls the body's members, so the mind rules and controls the feelings of the soul. In the neck, which towers over the other members and supplies to the limbs vital power, is expressed her loftiness, by which, presiding over the members of the Church, she unites the head to its body, for she unites Christ with the Church and the life which in the first place she received she pours forth on her other members. For it was fitting that just as death entered the world through a woman, so through a woman did life enter.* And as in Eve all died, so in Mary all rose again.* She—Eve—sinfully credulous of the serpent's words mixed the poisonous draught of death. She—Mary—bruising the serpent's head,* served to all the antitoxin of life, so she slew death and restored life.

*Cf. Rom 5:12
*1 Cor 15:22
*Gen 3:15

The hairs of her head are the thoughts of her heart, her ears the inner hearing. In her breast lies hid her secret and her thought stirs. Hence this custom has grown up that the guilty beat their breasts and, as it were, in striking accuse their own unrighteousness. By the breast therefore the secrets of that glorious breast are signified, by the arms the virtues of her works, by the hands the works themselves, by the fingers divers kinds of works. Her body is the undivided unity of her works, her thighs her desires, her feet her affections by which, entering upon the paths of justice, she has left behind clear footprints for those coming after.

Her feet are shod in the skins of dead beasts because they are protected by the examples of the Fathers who have gone before. The thighs are girt with the girdle of righteousness and with the belt of praise.* The body is clothed with that garment of which the Apostle says, 'As many of you as have been baptized in Christ have put on Christ.'* And he exhorts us to put on the new man who has been created after God in righteousness and the holiness of truth.*

*Is 11:5
*Gal 3:24
*Eph 4:24

Observe, man, and be amazed at a renewal so great, when Jeremiah says, 'The Lord will create a new thing upon the earth, a woman alone shall enclose a man.'* The same woman who enclosed has been enclosed. Enclosing the flesh, she has been enclosed by the Spirit. Enclosing the new man, she has been enclosed by the new man. Enclosing as generating, enclosed as regenerated. Generating in the

*Jer 31:22, cf. Bernard, Miss 2,8

shape of humanity, regenerated in the shape of renewal.

Let us pass on to the rest. Rings adorn her fingers because each one of her works shines forth in faith and love. Now a ring betokens faith and pure love. Her hands are beautifully shaped, golden, filled with hyacinths.* Beautiful because of the perfection of her work, golden because of the brightness of her wisdom, filled with hyacinths because of her pure and fervent intention. For the hyacinth, blue and red, reveals her shining and fervent work. **Sg 5:14*

Her arms are stamped with that seal of which the bridegroom says in the Canticle, 'Set me as a seal upon thy arm.'* Surely the fiery law covers the right hand and her left shines bright with the purple of the Lord's passion. From her ears hang the earrings of obedience, the fillet of discipline binds her hair, chains of purest and clearest thought adorn her breast, a golden necklace is at her throat. With this those in second place in kingdoms are wont to be crowned and this is the second crown. For the first gleams on the awesome head of the ruler of the whole world. The second has fallen to the lot of his mother. For she reigns uniquely in the kingdom of God and Christ.* Then under her and after her are the highest saints. **Sg 8:6* **Eph 5:5*

Her head is covered with the glory of her virginity and is veiled in the scarlet of charity. The blessing of the Lord is upon it and it is filled with the blessings of all nations.* It is crowned also with the crowns of all peoples and goes forth to the rejoicing of all. See in the beauty of her diadem the assembly of saints exulting in her quivering and reflecting light. See in the carved stones, the shining jewels, the glittering stars, the prophets awaiting her, the martyrs triumphant, confessors and virgins rejoicing. That crown is red with roses, white with lilies, pale with violets, green with laurels, heavy with palms, rich in oil, filled with every fruit, packed with every sweetness. **Gen 27:29*

Let it suffice that we have said these things, beloved, concerning the justification or adornment of the Virgin. It remains that by her holy leading we should be prepared to treat of deeper matters and more secret mysteries leading us to the vision of God.

HOMILY III

LORD, we have heard your works and we have been astounded.* We have pondered your marvels and we have fainted.* As your Word descended, our heart has been melted* and all our innermost being, trembling, has been laid bare to him. For while silence held all things and night in her journey reached her mid-course, your Almighty Word came from its royal abode.* You poured out, o Father, the tenderness of your love upon us* and you could no longer contain the multitude of your mercies.* You shed light in the darkness, dew upon the dryness and in the bitter frost you kindled a raging fire.

*Hab 3:2
*Cf. Ps 119:18
*Cf. Jos 7:5
*Wis 18:14-15
*Lk 1:78
*Ps 51:1

Your Son appeared to us as an abundance of food when grievous famine threatened, as a spring of living water to a life in distress and fainting from thirst in the heat. Or surely just as there is wont to appear a strong helper and deliverer for men beseiged,* who are about to rush out into battle with death before their eyes, with the enemy's threatening sword and his armed right hand thirsting for blood, so He appeared for us and became our salvation.*

*Cf. Ps 70:5, 71:7
*Is 12:2

Yet it is an excellent and salutary thing to recount again the beginning of our salvation and to treat of his incarnation, to recall whence he came, in what sort he descended, where and how he was conceived. We put last the manner of his conception so that following our plan through we may discuss more fully that ineffable union by which the womb of Blessed Mary bore fruit of the Holy Spirit. For though it be ineffable, yet much joy, a wondrous astonishing sweetness, can be richly drawn from it.

For there is the sum total of our faith, there the honor of our existence, the root of our life, the light of knowledge, the unbreakable bond of love and the door open to the eternal.

Now let blessed David present himself to us and tell us whence He came. His going forth was from the highest heaven.* What does 'from highest heaven' mean? From God, who is the supreme being, the highest good, the utmost blessedness.

*Ps 19:6

He is the supreme being who is neither limited by place nor subject to change nor enclosed within time. But he limits all things by the immensity of his majesty, moves all things mutable by his own immutability, encloses all times within the infinity of his eternity.

The supreme good is the same being, a being not derived from another, a good not from another good; not only because of the aforesaid immensity, immutability and eternity, but also because of the eternal bounty of the creation which it brought forth in time. And because of the infinite wisdom by which before anything was, it disposed all things in eternity. And because of the love ineffable by which his work was embraced before it was brought forth in creation.

Again, supreme blessedness consists in supreme good and by the reception of itself produces the truly blessed. For by participation in this blessedness eternal life is gained, perfect wisdom is granted, the fulness of love is possessed, so that there is complete freedom from care in eternity of life, full enjoyment in the light of wisdom, complete sanctity in the sweetness of love. These things we have said concerning supreme being, supreme good and supreme blessedness, that the height of heaven from which Christ came may shine upon us.

But because this highest heaven is the Father, the highest heaven the Word and the highest heaven the Holy Spirit, Christ came from the Father, he came also in a way from the Word, he came from the Holy Spirit. But in what way did he come from the Father, he who never left the Father? How from the Word, he who never ceased to be the Word? How from the

Holy Spirit when the Holy Spirit* proceeds from the Father and himself. This is a difficult question and demands deep thought. *reading spiritus for spiritu

And what shall be our path to these holy mysteries of God? In what order shall we complete the journey we have begun? Look, a thick mist and a luminous cloud impedes our ways. That water which holy Ezekiel saw issuing from the temple, covering not only his heels and knees but loins and neck, is poured over us to prevent our crossing.* Yet he in in whom we hope is present; in him we have from our youth up been taught to trust, that he would flood our souls and raise us above ourselves, setting our feet like harts' feet,* to bring us beyond our own heights, establishing for us a watch tower on the mount with Moses and Elijah* so that we may be able to behold with unveiled face that which we seek.* There shall be shown that it is good to be there; there we shall be more fully instructed concerning the vision of God.*

*Ez 47:1
*Hab 3:19, Ps 18:33
*Mt 17:3
*2 Cor 3:18
*Mt 17:4

But if we are willing to approach the darkness in which he himself is, having entered into the midst of the cloud,* stirred by the glory of such majesty, dismayed also by the immensity of that infinity, we shall not stand fast, we shall be as nothing. For God dwells in light inaccessible;* his fire devours the flesh like stubble;* his face no man can see and live.† The angels cannot fathom his depth; no power comes near to him except that which was united to the Word in the unity of Person. Therefore let us give glory to God and, falling on our faces, let us adore from afar the traces of the Trinity, believing in our hearts and confessing with our lips,* for whatever we have thought or said concerning him is less than he is.

*Ex 24:18
*1 Tim 6:16
*Is 5:24
†Ex 33:20
*Rom 10:10

Protected by this faith, let us turn back to solve the question before us. Christ has come from the Word, he has come from the Holy Spirit, since the whole Trinity accomplished his conception and his incarnation. For to come from the highest Trinity was no other than to be conceived and to become a human being by the same Trinity. Therefore it was said, 'His going forth is from the highest heaven.'*

*Ps 19:6

The Only-begotten came from the Father and from himself according to another kind of reasoning as well. He came from the Holy Spirit—in one way, however, from the Father and himself, in another way from the Holy Spirit.

Begotten of the Father eternally, begotten in time he came forth from his mother, remaining invisibly with the Father and dwelling visibly with men. For to go forth from the Father was this: to enter upon our world, to be seen openly, and to become what, from the nature of the Father, he was not. This indeed is wonderful, he came from him from whom he did not depart, going forth from him with whom he stayed, so that without intermission he was wholly in eternity, wholly in time; wholly was he found in the Father when wholly in the virgin, wholly in his own majesty and in his Father's at the time when he was wholly in our humanity.

If you ask how, gather the truth by means of an illustration. A word conceived in the heart goes forth complete in the voice, so that it comes perfectly to others, yet remains wholly in the heart. So the good Word spoken forth from the heart of the Father went forth into the broad plain, yet did not leave the Father.

The Word also came from himself and came down
Jn 1:14 beneath himself and dwelt among us, when he
Ph 2:7 emptied himself, taking the form of a servant. That
emptying was a descent. Yet he descended in such a way that he did not lose himself. He was made flesh in such a way that he did not cease to be the Word,
assumptio nor did the taking of humanity lessen the glory of
his majesty.

We must also know in what way he came from the Holy Spirit, since the Holy Spirit proceeds from him. The Holy Spirit indeed proceeds from him by an eternal procession, but he, born of the Virgin Mary, came from the Holy Spirit by a temporal conception. Concerning the eternal procession the psalmist says, 'By the word of the Lord were the heavens established and all the power of them
Ps 33:6 by the breath of his mouth'. The Word of the

Father he calls the mouth of the Lord, by which once God spoke to us.* He called the breath of his mouth Holy Spirit in that it comes forth from his mouth.

*Heb 1:2

*spirit = breath

That the Word came forth from the Holy Spirit, you have it thus in Habakkuk: 'God will come from the south wind and the holy one from Mount Paran.'* By 'south wind', in which is life-giving warmth and generative power, is meant the spirit which brings newness of life, making the seeds of virtue come forth. And though blessed Jerome, whom we desire to follow, calls Mount Paran the Father,* yet by Mount Paran the same Lord [the Holy Spirit] is meant. He is called mountain because of his preeminent charity, Paran because of the distribution of his graces. For 'Paran' is by interpretation 'division'. And the spirit of the Lord divides his gifts to each one as he wills.* Therefore, God came from the south wind, because he was conceived from a life-giving and regenerating warmth. He came from Mount Paran because he poured forth from an ineffable loftiness the divisions of charisms.

*Hab 3:3

*In Abac. 2; PL 25:1374B

*1 Cor 12:11

Tell us, holy Daniel, how he came down from this mountain. 'A stone,' he says, 'was cut without hands from the mountain.'* What stone? 'The stone which the builders rejected.'* A cornerstone, the stone which Jacob anointed, a stone in which there are seven eyes.* This was hewn without hands from the mountain, because the holy virgin conceived him not from a man nor by means of man, but by the Holy Spirit.

*Dan 2:34

*Ps 118:22

*Eph 2:20, Gen 28:18, Zach 3:9

Tell us also, blessed David, how he descended. 'He shall come down as rain upon the fleece, and as drops that water the earth.'* First one must say what this fleece is, what the earth [is], then how the rain descended on the fleece and how the drops watered the earth.

*Ps 72:6

A fleece, although it comes from the flesh, grows outside the flesh and knows not the sufferings of the flesh. By its softness, its homely color, it proclaims its gentleness and humility. Also, by being easy to handle it bears the mark of simplicity and innocence and with its natural covering it keeps warm the delicate limbs. It betokens the glorious Virgin, who dwelling in flesh, raised herself beyond the flesh and slew the passions of the flesh by the power of the Spirit. For she is known to have lived like no other in gentleness and humility. No one will be able adequately to describe her simplicity and innocence. The understanding does not grasp the charity by which she protects and unceasingly cherishes the human race.

Further, the aforesaid 'earth' points to the same Virgin, called 'earth' because of a certain likeness. For just as the old Adam was formed from an earth uncorrupt,* that had suffered no contagion, so the virgin soil brought forth from the earth a new Adam.

Gen 2:7

If you do not believe me when I proclaim the rising of the new man from the earth, believe the psalmist when he says 'truth has sprung from the earth'.* What greater newness [can there be] than the arising from the earth of the one who is the Truth? Believe also the trumpet of Isaiah as it produces a sweet and tuneful sound, saying 'drop down, O heavens, from above and let clouds rain upon the the just. Let the earth open and bring forth a Saviour.'* Again, he says, 'There will be a seed of the Lord in magnificence and glory and a lofty fruit of the earth.'* The seed of the Lord stood forth in magnificence and glory when, conceived by the Holy Spirit, sprung from the root of Jesse, it blossomed in full on the very top of the rod,* or rather it was the blossom. 'And the spirit of the Lord rested upon him, the spirit of wisdom and understanding, the spirit of counsel and strength, the spirit of knowledge and godliness, and the spirit of the fear of the Lord filled him.'* The fruit of the earth was raised on high because the blessed fruit of Mary was worthy to be lifted to the very heights of the godhead. We have said these things that we may show that the word 'earth' may be understood as Mary.

Ps 85:11

Is 45:8

Is 4:2

Cf. Ezk 7:10

Is 11:2-3

It remains to discuss how the rain descends upon the fleece and how the drops flow out over the earth.

The rain descends upon the fleece without sound, without movement, without any cleavage or division. It is gently poured out, peacefully received, sweetly drunk. Thus the drops gradually, little by little spread over the earth falling down so wonderfully and so gently that their coming is scarcely perceived and as they depart they bring forth the shoots. In the same way the rain coming from beyond, above the heavenly waters, came down into the Virgin's womb without human act, with no movement of concupiscence, her integrity unimpaired, her virgin's doors still locked. Gently was it poured, calmly received, ineffably made flesh. It came drop by drop upon her soil, unseen as it entered, and as it departed plainly going forth.

There are still other pictures of so great an event. For just as the sun's brightness penetrates glass without breaking it, and as a glance of the eyes plunges into calm clear water without parting or dividing it, while it opens up all things to their very depth, so the Word of God drew near the Virgin's dwelling and went forth from it, her virgin womb still closed. For he who might easily have created from nothing a body apart from the Virgin could easily draw without lesion of the flesh a body taken from the Virgin. For he did not submit to the law of nature but subjected the law of nature to himself.

We have told how the Word of God came down. Where he came down is made clear in like manner, for he came down into the Virgin's womb, a womb unstained, unspotted, hallowed by the touch of divine unction. There, united to our flesh, made akin to our nature, he wrought a most holy and secret mystery, that the two might be in the one flesh and enjoy the one dwelling.* **Cf. Gen 2:24*

Therefore the invisible God was made visible man, the impassible and immortal showed himself passible and mortal. He who was not confined within the garments of our substance willed to be so confined. There is enclosed within the womb of a mother one whose immensity encloses the whole range of heaven and earth. And Mary's body enfolds him whom the heaven of heavens does not contain.

If you ask how it was done, hear the archangel
setting forth the plan to Mary, and saying to her,
'The Holy Spirit shall come upon you and the power
Lk 1:35 of the Most High shall overshadow you.' Rejoice
therefore and be glad, Mary, for you will conceive by
a breath. Rejoice, for you will be found pregnant by
Mt 1:18 the Holy Spirit. You had indeed been betrothed to
Joseph, but you were forestalled by the Holy Spirit.
He who created you marked you and claimed you for
himself. He who fashioned you himself became your
spouse; he became the lover of your beauty, he who
fashioned it. He himself calls you, saying 'Come, my
friend, my fair one, my dove. For now the winter is
Sg 2:10-11 past and departed. Come.' He desired your beauty†
†Cf. Ps 45:11 and longed to join you to himself. Impatient of
delay, he hastens to come to you.

Cf. Is 52:1 Rise, therefore, put on your garments of glory.
Adorn yourself with your precious jewels, for the
Is 62:4 Lord has pleasure in you. Rise to meet your bride-
groom and your God and say to him, 'Behold, the
Lk 1:38 handmaid of the Lord'. Hasten, delay not, for he
Hab 2:3 will not tarry but will rejoice as a giant to run his
Ps 19:5 course. Do you hasten too, forget your own people
Ps 45:10 and your father's house, run to meet him that you
Sg 1:1 may be kissed with the kiss of God and be caught
up in his blessed embrace.

Go forth, for already the bridal couch has been
placed and the bridegroom comes to you, the Holy
Spirit comes. He will come upon you and the power
Lk 1:35 of the Most High will overshadow you. Suddenly,
while you do not hope for it, while you grieve for
the ills of delay and are distressed by the absence of
the beloved, swiftly and suddenly he will come upon
you that you may enjoy unexpected bliss and be
overwhelmed with a new gladness.

He will come not only upon you but into you, that he may see you more closely and breathe into you a grateful love, bringing into you with an intimate bedewing the good word, the word full of happiness and wonder, full of counsel, full of joy, full of salvation. 'The Holy Spirit will come upon you,' that at his touch your womb may tremble, your belly swell, your spirit rejoice, your stomach expand. 'Be blest', that is, increase the more,* you who enjoy such sweetness, you are worthy of such a heavenly kiss, you are united to such a spouse, you are made fruitful by such a bridegroom.

*macta *i.e.* magis aucta

'The Holy Spirit shall come upon you.' He has come to others of the saints, he will come to others, but he comes more to you, for he chose you before and above all others, that you may surpass all those who have been before or after you or shall be in the fulness of grace.

He filled Abel with such innocence that, pure in deed and gentle at heart,* he suffered death at his brother's hand.* But your innocence has restored thousands of guilty ones to innocence and salvation. He translated Enoch,* but the flesh which you will bear, when it has been taken up from the earth, will draw all things to itself.* He filled Abraham with faith and an obedience that should profit his descendants,* but, saved by your faith and obedience, the whole world gives thanks. He filled Moses and he appointed him to be the one to bring the Law,* not grace, but you are the one bringing not only the Giver of the Law but the Bestower of grace and glory.* He appointed David prophet and king,* but David writes for you and calls your Son his Lord.* Why should I say more? You surpass all, you rank not only before all humanity but even before heaven's highest powers.

*Ps 24:4
*Gen 4:8
*Gen 5:24
*Jn 12:32
*Gen 22
*Ex 19
*Jn 1:17
*1 Sam 16
*Ps 110:1

Hence you will inherit a name more glorious than theirs. For while one is called 'angel of God', another 'prophet', another 'herald' and each is valued according to his name, in proportion to his rank and dignity, you will be called by the unique and special name 'Mother of God', and therefore mother of salvation, mother of grace, mother of mercy.

'The Holy Spirit will come upon you.' He will come in fertility, in abundance, in fulness, in the outpouring of flesh and spirit. And when he has filled you, he will still be over you and will be borne upon your waters to create in you a better and a greater wonder than when in the beginning he was borne upon the waters to bring creation to beauty and shape.*

**Gen 1:2*

'And the power of the Most High shall overshadow you.' Christ, the power and the wisdom of God* shall overshadow you. He will take from you his humanity and in the taking of the flesh he will keep the fulness of the divinity* which you could not carry. He will overshadow you because the humanity taken by the Word will expose itself to the light inaccessible and that light, controlled by the exposure, will flood your chaste body.

**1 Cor 1:24*

**Col 1:19*

Pleasant is it, beloved, to linger awhile amidst such solemnity of joy and to inquire a bit about the aforesaid conception. Pleasant it is, addressing her, to question the divine enclosure, the most precious and holy vessel in which the Word of God was conceived.

We pray you therefore, Lady, most worthy Mother of God, not to scorn those who seek in fearfulness, ask in piety, knock in love.* We ask, by what feeling you were moved, by what affection held, by what incitement stirred when these things took place in you and you conceived the Word made flesh. Where was your soul, your heart, your mind, your feeling, your reason? You were on fire like the bush which once was shown to Moses and you were not burnt up.* Being melted, you burned with supernal fires. Melted in the fire, you took strength from the fire so that you even burned and again you melted.

**Cf. Mt 7:7-8*

**Ex 3:2*

The fire revealed a shining dew, the shining dew produced an anointing, the anointing furnished the holy seed by which Abraham was promised that in it all nations should be blessed.* You have clung, beauteous virgin, in close embrace to the author of beauty and were made more a virgin, indeed more than a virgin, because mother and virgin, you received by the inpouring of God this holy seed. Therefore hail, full of grace, the Lord is with you.* Blessed are you among women and blessed the fruit of your womb.*

**Gen 22:17-18*

**Lk 1:28*

**Lk 1:42*

HOMILY IV

YESTERDAY, beloved, our discourse—concerned with spiritual union and the virgin conception—is hastening towards the birth, so that we declare that she whom we know to have conceived by the Holy Spirit brought forth true God and man. For in labor she brought forth the Son of God, so that God came down into her body wondrously deeming her worthy, wondrously and incredibly loving her, and in the flesh that he took he visited the orphaned sons of Adam.

Therefore the Son of God was made the son of man. In unity of the person he was God and man: God of the substance of the Father, begotten before the world; man of the substance of his mother, born in the world. So, a giant of twin substance, he rejoiced to sing with tuneful voice and sweet airs to the lyre of our body and on the organ made of our flesh to send forth dulcet sounds to re-echo as it were with ineffable harmony, so that he raised up stones, moved trees, drew wild beasts, led forth on high men delivered from their flesh.

For by the sweetness of his wonderful song he raised up from stones sons of Abraham and the trees of the wood, that is the hearts of the Gentiles, he moved to faith.* Wild beasts also, that is fierce **Mt 3:9* passions and savage barbarism, he tamed to good ways and he set among the gods men drawn from among men. Well did David, whose songs echo to the ends of the earth, fulfil the role of singer, for from his stock was that greater precentor to be born.

But now let us see how the blessed virgin gave him

birth. She bore him with her virginity untouched, because she conceived him with her modesty preserved. She was inviolate when she brought him forth, untouched as she conceived him. And him whom she conceived without sin she gave birth to without pain. Having no contact in her conception, she suffered no tearing at his birth. For if (what is wrong to imagine) she had conceived him in the lust of the flesh, doubtless she would suffer pain at his
=RB 7:33 birth, as Scripture says, 'lust involves pain'.*

Our first parent [Eve], disregarding the true and eternal joy which she could have enjoyed by the love and contemplation of God, fell, weakened by the dissolute lust of the flesh and through shameful intemperance she endured the ills of suffering and the stings of cruel death. Hence comes it that to this day the daughters of Eve bring forth in pain and what they conceived in delight they put forth with great bitterness of the flesh.

But not only they, but all the sons of Adam who delight in the flesh, are tormented in the flesh, so that the source of their torment is their delight. And they experience in pain what they had previously taken with delight and they learn not to love the flesh nor to fulfil its desires. 'For he who has sown in the flesh,' says the Apostle, 'shall from the flesh
Gal 6:8 reap corruption.'* Further, the Mother of God, not delighted by the flesh nor tormented in the flesh, was the more virgin by her conception and was the stronger by giving birth at the hand of that midwife concerning which the psalmist said to God, 'Let it be
Ps 119:73 Your hand that saves me'.*

The only-begotten of the Father is called the
Heb 1:2 hand of God, through whom he made the world.* This hand, having been made, when it became incarnate not only inflicted no wound upon the mother but, as the prophet bears witness, itself bore our
Is 53:4 griefs and carried our sorrows.* Clearly that hand was full of remedies, full of medicines; it healed every ill, drove away deaths and awakened those that were dead, broke up the gates of hell, bound the strong one and stripped him of his armor, opened the

heavens and poured out the spirit of charity upon the hearts of his own.* That hand looses those that are bound, enlightens the blind, raises those struck down, loves the righteous, protects strangers, supports the orphan and the widow.* It snatches the tempted from temptation, restores with consolation those who sorrow, brings back joy to the sad, protects under its shadow those who toil, writes for those who reflect upon the laws, touches and blesses the hearts of those who pray, that by its touch they may be strengthened in love, by its blessing they may make progress and persevere in their work. And thereafter he brings them back to their fatherland and leads them to the Father.

*Mt 4:23-4 & 12:29

*Ps 146:8

For this cause was the Word made flesh, that by the flesh it might draw the flesh and that joining flesh to flesh by the bond of charity it might bring back the wandering sheep to the invisible things of God and to the invisible omnipotent Father.* Because deserting God, that sheep fell in the flesh it needed by the mystery of this incarnate hand to be lifted up and returned to the Father as in a sort of carriage.

*Cf. Lk 15:5-6

Therefore with this midwife hand, Mary not only felt no pain but remained virgin even in giving birth. She is the door concerning which we read in the book of Ezekiel: that door will remain closed for the prince and through it the prince will go forth.* Through this door Christ, prince of the kings of the earth,*indeed has issued and just as in entering he did not open it, so in leaving he did not unclose it. He passed through in peace, and his path was not seen.

*Ezk 44:2-3

*Rev 1:5

But if you marvel that God was born while Mary's womb remained closed and sealed with her virgin purity, marvel also that though the door of the sepulchre was closed and sealed, he returned to the upper world, and when the doors were locked came in to his disciples.* For we are not removing your wonder, but keeping at bay your unbelief.

*Jn 20:19

Whatsoever he willed, the Lord did,* and all his works may be wondered at but not examined. 'All things are difficult,' said Solomon, 'and man cannot explain them in words.'* For, not to mention how

*Ps 135:6

*Qo 1:8

from one small grain a mighty forest of trees arises and how from the seed of Adam and Eve was produced the mass of humanity, who would explain the springing of insects from the earth? Whence came the spreading of their wings, the march of their feet? Whence the eyes and shape of the head? Whence the shape of the body? Whence the sting so fine that sometimes it disappears from the sight? It is so hollow and pierced that when the blood has been taken in the tiny body of a creature so short-lived is filled.

But if your reason collapses at the examination of an insect, o man, be ashamed to search into matters higher than yourself and to track down matters stronger than you. If you do not reflect on yourself and the depth of your soul, how do you rise to the infinite majesty? How will the man who does not know how to count to the first number be able to judge of arithmetic? Will the man who does not know what a point is or a line be proficient in geometry? Will the one who does not know how to utter a sound be able to teach music? Will the man be a skilled astronomer who does not know what movement is? So he who does not know himself does not penetrate the deep things of God.

Yet what is human wisdom compared with the wisdom of God? It holds in its presence neither the place of a point nor the point of a point. If I may put forward a surprising idea, the insect's eye can be compared somewhat proportionally with the immensity of heaven, but the measure of man is out of all proportion to the divine immensity. What part in infinity has the finite, the measurable in the immeasurable, that which lasts but a moment with the eternal? Or by what multiplication or number will the creature be compared with the Creator? If you stretch a thousand thousand into infinity, you will exhaust yourself in fruitless toil, and not even in the very smallest proportion will you be able to compare human knowledge with divine wisdom.

If therefore the being of God is reflected upon, there will not be found the substance of man.

Witness the prophet, who says, 'All the peoples are in your presence as though they are not and are counted as a moment and mere emptiness.'* And the Lord said to Moses, 'This will you say to the sons of Israel: "He who is has sent me to you." '* When he said that he is, he took away being from others.

**Is 40:17*

**Ex 3:14*

Therefore believe God, human insignificance—or rather the nothingness of humans—and let the firm foundation of your reasoning be upon All powerful wisdom. Set that forth, take up that and from that draw your conclusion.

Believe that all those who attach themselves perfectly to their Creator will not be thwarted by the law of nature but will be established above nature by nature's Creator. Nature did not impose its law upon its Creator but the Creator gave to nature the laws he willed. And when he wills, he changes the laws themselves, as when he made wine from water and fashioned eyes from clay.* When too, holding his very self in his hands he shared it with his disciples to be eaten and drunk,* remaining wholly outside them and feeding inwardly those who ate it. So, as to the argument, he went forth from the closed womb of the Virgin. These things have been said against the unbelievers and for the benefit of unbelievers.

**Jn 2:11, 9:6*

**Cf. Mt 26:26*

I will not leave untouched you, the Jews, who killed the prophets sent to you and slaughtered the Son of God who had come for your salvation,* mixing the same cup for the Lord of the prophets as you had mixed before for the prophets. For you said, 'This is the heir. Let us kill him and the inheritance will be ours.'* But because you killed the heir, you lost the inheritance. No longer should it be called your inheritance. You lost it after the space of a thousand years.

**Cf. Mt 23:37*

**Mt 21:38*

Why then do you say that the Messiah has not yet come, that the Christ has not yet been born? Either you yourselves are lying or you make a liar of the Truth which speaks in the psalm concerning David, saying, 'I will establish his seed for ever and his

**Ps 89:29* throne as the days of heaven'.* And again, 'I have
sworn once by my holiness [I will not lie to David];
his seed shall remain for ever and his throne as the sun
in my sight and as the moon for ever full, and as a
**Ps 89:35-7* faithful witness in heaven.'* I ask you: where is that
promise? Where is that throne of David, perfect as the
sun in the sight of God and lasting as the days of
heaven? But the Truth does not deceive nor is he
deceived, especially when blessed Jacob says, 'The
scepter shall not be removed from Judah nor the
leader from his loins until he that is to be sent shall
**Gen 44:10* come and he will be the expectation of the nations.'*
Come to the Church of God and you will see the Son
and Lord of David sitting on his throne with great
power and majesty.

But if you still shamelessly and irrationally contend and say, 'When Christ comes our race will reign
with him,' look at the primitive Church sprung from
your race. See your brothers, how they reign with
**Si 39:14* Christ. See their hearts live for ever.* Peoples tell of
their wisdom and the whole Church of the saints
proclaims their praise. Tribes and nations beseech
them and the sons of their mother, that is the
Church, bow before them. Blush therefore, enemies
of Christ, to be trodden beneath the feet of him to
whom it was said by the Father, 'Sit on my right
**Ps 110:1* hand until I make your enemies your footstool',*
and begin to be among his members that you may
drink the blood of salvation which your fathers
poured out to their own destruction.

And what shall I say concerning you gentiles? You
**Cf. Gen 2:23* are our flesh and bone.* This makes us more anxious
concerning your salvation. Why do you not believe
that Christ is God? You believe indeed that he was
born and that, being born of the Virgin, he lived
without sin. But because you do not believe that he is
God, you make a dangerous mistake and sin to your
own destruction. But you say, 'We have been taught
so to believe by our prophet.' If you wish to know
that that prophet of yours was false, we condemn
him from his own words and from his own lips
reprove his folly. He said that Christ was truly born

of the Virgin, that he lived free from falsehood or any sin. But Christ, who according to this testimony was always truthful, claimed openly in the Gospel—prophets and apostles bearing him witness—that he was God and the Son of God. Therefore he was a liar who maintained that Christ was not God.

For refuge therefore betake your very selves to the catholic and apostolic Church; for just as once, in the flood, no place of safety was found but the ark of Noah,* so now there is no place of refuge but the Church of Christ. **Gen 7*

Leaving these matters aside, let us return to our subject and let us weigh carefully the difference between the child-bearing of Mary and that of Eve. Eve bore a child, being corrupt. Mary brought forth, being incorrupt. Eve in pain, Mary in health. Eve in the 'old man', Mary in the new. Eve brought forth a slave, Mary a Lord. Eve a guilty one, Mary a righteous one. Eve a sinner, Mary one who justifies from sin. The childbearing of Eve multiplies deaths, that of Mary saves from death. While Eve gives birth, the dragon lies in wait. At Mary's child-bearing angels minister. Terror of heart seizes upon Eve in labor, but as Mary brings forth divine power gladdens her.

Those, Eve, whom you brought forth you expose to many misfortunes. Your offspring, Mary, you save from all evil. As Eve gave birth, malice abounded, but when Mary did grace superabounded. The heavens were glad, earth exulted when Mary gave birth and hell was troubled and aghast. The heavens in their joy produced a shining star and a glorious army of angels, uttering praise and saying 'Glory to God in the highest and on earth peace to men of good will.'* **Lk 2:14* The earth exulting brought shepherds giving glory and magi adoring and offering gifts, gold, frankincence and myrrh.* **Cf. Mt 2:1-11* Hell, disturbed, brought the wicked king and moved to rage his minions to stir them to the slaughter of the innocents, with no pity for the unborn, and killing those they snatched from the breasts.* **Mt 2:16-18* So at Mary's childbearing the good rejoiced, and the wicked were dismayed, for he was being born who would render good things to the good and strike the evil with the vengeance they deserved.

Consider that when the mother gave birth, the face of the universe smiled and the glad world applauded its Lord. Reflect that the clouds were swept away and the sky put on its beauty and the
Bar 3:35 stars, saying 'here we are', blazed with joy for him. Reflect that night poured forth light in the darkness and instead of blackness offered radiance that night gave light before the sun arose and a brightness which from its exceeding brilliance obscured the splendor of the sun. Concerning this night the psalmist says
Ps 139:11 'Night is my light in my delights' and turning to the Lord he follows and says, 'The darkness will not be dark with you and the night will be as bright as the
Ps 139:12 day,' for his darkness is as his light.

Pleasant and clear shone the warmth of the air and all things in peace bore witness in their order that the author of peace and sweetness had come. Do you not think that at the birth of Christ the whole world was at peace when you read that at his death it was thrown into confusion? Would all things be troubled at his death and not be in peace at his birth? Would they perceive in their senses that he was dying and not know that he was being born?

If all things rejoiced at his birth, how did his mother rejoice? If all things were glad, how great a gladness did she enjoy? What happiness was in the mother if all things were so glad? The tongue falters, the heart fails, the mind is aghast at the weight of a joy so great. For how could so frail a vessel, still made of clay and mortal, hold out before such mighty joys? For at the birth of Christ he overshadowed her who overshadowed her at his conception. He gave her the power to bear the joys, who granted her their wealth, and the strength of his divinity with wondrous power controlled her whom the glory of his majesty filled with unspeakable richness.

When therefore she had brought forth the promised Son and had given birth to the day from day for our day, turning to God with her whole heart she gave voice to her thanks and praise on high, offered the acceptable sacrifice of her lips and offered the sacrifice of her jubilation,* gave the peaceful holocaust of her heart and for a burnt offering to the Lord sacrificed the sweet perfumed incense.* Taking up the new-born Emmanuel, she beheld a light incomparably fairer than the sun and saw a fire that water cannot quench. She received in the covering of the flesh she had borne the light that lightens all things and she was worthy to carry in her arms the Word that carries the universe. Filled therefore with the knowledge of God as the waters of the sea when they overflow, she is carried outside herself and with heart raised on high she stands still in deepest contemplation. She marvels that she, a virgin, has become a mother and with joy marvels that she is the Mother of God. She knows that in her have been fulfilled the promise of the patriarchs, the oracles of the prophets and the longings of the fathers of old, who foretold that Christ would be born of a virgin and with all their prayers awaited his birth.

*Cf. Ps 27:6

*Cf. Dt 27:7, Lev 4:31

She sees the Son of God given to her and rejoices that the world's salvation is entrusted to her. She hears him speaking to her and the Lord God saying in her 'Behold I chose you from all flesh* and made you blessed among all women.* See, I have entrusted to you my Son, committed to you my only Son. Fear not to suckle the one you have borne, to train up the one you have brought forth. Know him not only as your Lord but as your Son. He is my Son by his divinity, your son by the humanity he has taken.'

*Si 45:4

*Lk 1:28

With what feeling and eagerness, with what humility and reverence, with what love and devotion then did she fulfil this task is unknown to men, but known to God, who searches the reins and the heart and who weighs the soul.*

*Ps 7:9 & Pr 16:2

Often, as we believe, forgetting to eat and drink, disdaining the needs of the flesh, she spent sleepless nights that she might think in her spirit upon Christ, might see in the flesh Christ from whom she was on fire with longing, whom she was on fire to serve. Often also she did what was written in the Canticles: 'I sleep and my heart keeps watch.'* For asleep in the flesh she was awake in the spirit, dreaming in the

*Sg 5:2

quiet of night of him whom day by day she thought upon, waking she found herself in him, and yielding **Cf. Ps 4:8* her limbs to slumber she rested sleeping in peace.*

**Mt 6:21* Where her treasure was, there was her heart also.* Where her glory was, there also was her conscience. She loved her Lord and her Son with all her heart, with all her mind, with all her strength, with all her **Mt 22:37* heart,* because with complete affection. With all her mind because with her whole understanding, with all her strength because with the whole purpose of her heart and the carrying out of all his commandments. She saw with her eyes and with her hands **Cf. 1 Jn 1:1* handled the Word of life.* Happy she to whom it was given to cherish him who cherishes and nourishes all things, to carry him who carries the universe, to suckle a son who pours milk into the breasts, to feed him **Cf. Ps 147:9* who feeds all things and provides food for the birds.*

The Wisdom of the Father clung round her neck and in her arms rested the Power that moves all **Cf. 1 Cor 1:24* things.* The little Jesus stood on his mother's lap and **Cf. Mt 11:29* in her virgin bosom rested that rest of holy souls.* Sometimes tilting his head while she held him with right hand or left, he bent his gentle gaze upon his **1 P 1:12* mother, he whom angels longed to look upon,* and called her mother with sweet murmur, he whom every spirit calls in time of need.

Filled with the Holy Spirit she clasped the sacred breast of her Son to her own breast and pressed his face to hers. Sometimes she kissed his hands and arms and trustingly, with a mother's privilege, took sweet kisses from his sacred mouth. She was not sated with beholding him nor satisfied with hearing him. Him many kings and prophets desired to see and saw **Lk 10:24* not, and to hear and heard not.*

She progressed further and further in love, and her spirit burning in her ever wakeful soul was fixed upon his divine glances. For love of her Son she feared neither toil nor grief nor dangers nor poverty nor want, neither terrors nor death nor the rage of the wicked king, the flight and return from Egypt. She was most pleasing in her activity, full of joy in what she did, prompt in obedience, devoted in her service, humble in her submission. In everything she acted with success; she ordered all things vigorously and wisely. With countenance serene and tranquil mind she accomplished all the duties of humanity. For as she was unlike any other in contemplation, so also in the active life she found no equal.

Where does this discourse lead? We are defeated and are glad to be defeated. We have attempted what is far above us, we are lying far below. Let us therefore return to ourselves and wash away our sins with weeping. Let us ask the Mother of pity to grant us, by the hidden joys and unspeakable love which by unique privilege she earned, the desire for her motherly love and to plead with her Son for our sins.

At the end of the discourse the reader will know that four homilies remain in the order in which the last four steps in the ascent of Blessed Mary have been put forward. The first will tell the suffering and the sword which the glorious one endured when Christ was dying. The second will explain the glory she felt when he arose. The third will be of her assumption and exaltation. The fourth will treat of the fulness of perfection which she will have one day, we hope with us and from us.

HOMILY V

REMEMBERING our promise and knowing that we can do nothing of ourselves, for we are not in anything sufficient of ourselves,* we pray the Father of lights* to enlighten our hearts and to open our lips.

*2 Cor 3:5

*Jas 1:17

We must know that there are two kinds of martyrdom, the one clearly seen, the other secret; the one hidden; the one in the flesh, the other in the spirit. In the flesh the holy apostles and martyrs suffered. They spent themselves for their love of truth and their witness to Jesus, and having become Christ's victim they drank the cup of the Lord,* that by the cross they might mount to glory and by a death in time they might be worthy to be made partakers of eternal life. It is they who in the Song of Songs climb the palm tree to seize the fruit* and by the crimson ascent are gathered into the litter of the true Solomon, so that they recline on a golden couch and are enriched with delights of every kind,* eating and drinking in the kingdom of God,* Christ ministering to them.

*Cf. Mt 20:22

*Sg 7:8

*Sg 3:10

*Lk 22:30

But those saints suffered in the spirit who in their spirit endured something more cruel than suffering in the flesh. In spirit Abraham suffered when, being bidden to sacrifice his only son Isaac whom he loved, he was deeply moved by his fatherly love and was stirred to the depth of his heart by his affection for his son.* Nevertheless as a diligent workman he performed the task laid upon him and, hastening to obey the divine command, he reached in a three days' journey Mount Horeb. There, as commanded, he put

*Gen 22

together the heap of wood, bound Isaac and laid him upon it. He seized his knife and would have slain his son had he not been checked by a voice from heaven and heard 'Stretch not your hand against the lad. Now **Gen 22:12* I know you fear God.'* That man suffered more than in the flesh because he did not hesitate to offer in faith and devotion the son whom he loved more than his own flesh and finally on that third day showed he was fully intent upon the deed.

Similarly Moses suffered in the spirit when he **Ps 106:23* stood in the breach before the face of God* and prepared to pray for the safety of his people. He cast far away his own safety, saying, 'either drive away this plague from them or blot me out from the book **Ex 32:31-2* you have written'.* What a dart in the heart! What a blow inflicted on the very depths of the soul! 'Either drive away this plague from them or blot me out from the book you have written.' He chose to be **Rom 9:3* anathema, far from Christ, on behalf of his brothers,* and considering the safety of others his own, he was more distressed for another's loss than for his own. He did not believe life would be complete for him if he lived while others died and if he alone entered the kingdom while others were in danger. For charity **1 Cor 13:5* seeks not its own,* because it places the common good before its own, not its own before the common good.

For this reason David too suffered in the spirit when he saw the angel slaying the people and he groaned and, turning in his heart to God, he said that he had sinned and done evil and he prayed that the **2 Sam 24:17* sword might be turned against himself.* He excuses Israel and demands that he be destroyed, with his stock, provided that the sword dripping blood might cease from slaughter and the avenging wrath no longer destroy the innocent. From these examples, I think, we see that the martyrdom of the spirit goes beyond the torments of the flesh.

Therefore the glorious lady [Mary], triumphing in this kind of suffering, the more glorious as she was nearer them all, clung to the revered cross of the Lord's passion, drained the cup, drank the passion and, having quaffed the torment of grief, was able to endure a grief unlike any other. She hastens after Jesus not only for the scent of his perfumes,* but in the abundance of his sorrows. Not only [does she follow] for the joy of his consolations but also for the wealth of his sufferings. His mother perceived the true Solomon in the diadem with which she had crowned him* and she, herself crowned with the crown of affliction, followed after him.

**Cf. Sg 1:3*

**Sg 3:11*

She stood near the cross* that she might see her son's sweet head anointed with oil above his fellows',* beaten with rods, and crowned with thorns—heart-rending sight! She saw there was neither form nor beauty in him who was lovely with a beauty beyond the sons of men.* She saw him who was high above all nations despised and of no reputation,* the holy of holies crucified with criminals and malefactors, the eyes of the lofty man brought low, the head of the sustainer of all things sagging to his shoulders, the radiant face of God wither away and the glory of his countenance hidden.

**Jn 19:25*

**Ps 45:7*

**Ps 45:2*

**Is 53:2-3*

Therefore to him it was said by the prophet: 'Truly you are a hidden God.'* Why hidden? Because he had neither form nor beauty,* yet power was in his hands. There [in his hands] was hidden his fortitude.* Was he not hidden when he submitted his hands to things powerful* and his palms received the nails? The print of the nails gleamed on his hands and his innocent side received the wound. They shackled his feet in fetters, the iron pierced his soles* and his feet were fastened to the tree. These wounds did God suffer on our behalf at the hands of his own people, in his own home.

**Is 45:15*

**Is 53:2*

**Hab 3:4*

**Pr 31:19*

**Cf. Ps 105:18*

O how marvellous are his wounds, by which the wounds of the world were healed! How victorious his wounds, by which he slew death and stung hell. 'Death,' he says, 'I will be your death. I will be your sting, o hell.'* Leviathan was caught on the hook† and while he opens his mouth to eat the worm that cried out in the psalm 'I am a worm and no man',* he halted, wounded with the iron [sword] of those wounds. With these precious wounds was the

**Hos 13:14*

†Cf. Job 40:20, Gregory the Great, Moralia *33,7; PL 76:680C*

**Ps 22:6*

devil snared and man set free.

Therefore, o Church, o dove, you have coverts
**Sg 2:14* in the rock and a hollow in the wall in which to rest.*
**1 Sam 17* Fear not raging Goliath,* the cruel-hearted, by his
countenance uttering mighty threats, since he has been robbed of his strength with his own sword by the true David. He wished to strike and he found a striker. He sought to wound and himself was grievously wounded. He tied himself up in his own knots and was thrown down by his own effort. He seized upon what was not his and lost what belonged to him. He attacked another's and lost his own.

The blood of Christ was weighed in the balance, and in the Father's judgement proving the heavier, it destroyed the sins of men and the devil's chains. Therefore being despoiled alike of his most cherished vessels and of everything in which he boasted and of the weapons in which he trusted, the ancient foe is reserved for the judgement and will pay the penalty for ever for having poured out the blood of the Son of God. And you, ungrateful Jews, blasphemers, parricides, you will burn with him, so that he will have as companions in the fire those whom he found to help him in his crime.

The Lord says, 'I have nourished and raised up
**Is 1:2* sons, but they have contemned and despised me.'* In
truth, he nourished and raised you up, and through
your wickedness he was raised upon the cross. He
**2 Sam 1:24* clothed you in scarlet in the delights* and beauty of
glory, and by your madness he was stripped naked.
**Pr 4:9* A glorious crown protected you,* and upon his head
you set a crown of thorns. He fed you with the flour
**Ps 147:14* of wheat* and to him you gave gall to eat. He says:
'they gave me gall to eat and when I was thirsty they
**Ps 69:21* gave me vinegar to drink.'* He lengthened the cords
of your inheritance and strengthened the pegs [of
**Is 54:2* your tents],* but you stretched out his arms, and
fastened with nails the hands that raised your dead.

At this the sky was aghast and clothed itself with darkness as with a hair shirt. Sun and moon withdrew their light and were surrounded with grief. They were seen to weep for their Creator. The air was blackened and ringed about with thick darkness. The earth trembled and shook.* Rocks were rent, graves were opened and from hell the dead arose.* Hell itself shuddered at the crime and hell's furies were dismayed. But the Jews, more unfeeling than the earth, harder than the rocks, more cruel than hell, more unbelieving than the demons, neither perceived the Lord nor broke his heart nor shuddered at his crime nor exercised his faith.

**Ps 77:18*
**Cf. Mt 27:45-52*

And what will you do, o wicked people, sinful race, house that shed the blood of the crucified, when he comes in the clouds with great power and majesty?* He will come down with heaven and earth ablaze, and by the terror of his coming he will dissolve the elements; and when he has come, the sign of the cross will be seen in the sky, and the beloved one will show the scars of his wounds and the prints of the nails by which he was transfixed in his own home.

**Mt 24:30*

Then you will weep over yourself, with lamentation as for an only son.* You will say to the mountains 'cover us' and to the hills 'fall upon us'* before the sword of the dove* and before the anger of God's wrath. He will set you in a furnace of fire on the day of his appearing, in his anger he will confound you, and the fire will devour you.* A raging whirlwind will seize you, a fierce tempest will drown you, unending fire will burn you and the chaos of hell will enfold you, as—too late—you offer your prayer. And do not say, as you are wont, 'he prophesies for a distant day'.* Behold, the Lord causes you to be carried away as a barnyard cock is carried off, and he will remove you* like a worn garment†, so that despised and an exile, you will die in a land not your own and, worn out by a double contrition,* you will, through distress alone, regain the knowledge you lost and learn by your punishment what in your sin you presumed upon.

**Cf. Jer 6:26*
**Lk 23:30*
**Jer 46:16*
**Ps 21:9*
**Ezk 12:27*
**reading* sublevabit *for* sublevavit
†Is 22:17
**Jer 17:18*

Therefore the heart of the glorious Virgin, burned with unspeakable sorrow equally for the death of her son and the loss of the Jews and pierced with a great dart of pity, sighed in deep anguish. She drained a cup more bitter than death itself and that which the human race could not endure, she—a woman—was strong enough to bear, assisted by the grace of God. She overcame her sex, she overcame human nature, and she suffered beyond what was human. She was more tortured than if she was suffering torture in herself, since she loved infinitely more than herself the source of her grief.

And to leave out for a while that bitter grief for the death of her son, who would describe with what sorrow the blessed Virgin was racked, with what anguish pressed, when with the eye of prophecy she saw the condemnation of most of her own race, the blotting out of the nation and the overthrow of the once holy city of Jerusalem? Certainly the prophets, knowing the future, had foretold the destruction of the Jews and with many tears followed
Lk 19:41 their ruin. The Lord himself wept over Jerusalem and the apostles long mourned their country's treachery. Paul, filled with pity, desired to be anathema from Christ for the sake of his brethren
Rom 9:3 according to the flesh, that he might rouse them to their salvation and to emulation. How much more would the mother of pity do everything, willingly bear everything, expose herself to whatever pains, even to death, that she might remove from her race the destruction and disaster that threatened it. But
Ps 99:4 the king's honor loves justice and the undeniable justice of the high God most justly arranged that over which the gracious mother of the Redeemer wept in her pity.

Let no one argue that the Jews were hateful to the Mother of God for their having condemned her Son to a most shameful death. For those whom she saw near to eternal death she in no way considered to deserve her hatred and insult, but to deserve great affection, many tears, and a great pity. Therefore sharing in the charity as well as in the cross of Jesus, she took up her prayer for them and with her whole heart, beating on the ears of the Father's pity, said, 'Father, forgive them this sin, for they do not know
Lk 23:34 what they are doing'. This, his utterance, was her

desire, that the more effectively the ears of the unconfined spirit who fills and hears all things everywhere might be beaten upon.

For the rest, whoever you are who love the Mother of God, take note and reflect with all your innermost feelings [upon her] who wept for the Only-begotten as he died, and on what was demanded of her. The grief she felt in the passion of her son goes beyond all understanding, goes beyond man's comprehension. No simile, no comparison comes near such bitter grief.

For what mother loved her son as she did? Not by chance did she, like other women, conceive him, but the only Son of the Father entered his mother's womb by loving choice and free bounty. This is why she loved him more. Nor did he bring, as others do, any pain to his mother in his life, but he poured upon her abundance of grace, as the Scripture says of him: 'He did no sin nor was guile found in his mouth.'* **1 Pet 2:22* Again, concerning grace: 'Handsome with a loveliness beyond the sons of men, grace has been poured upon your lips, because God has blessed you for ever.'* **Ps 45:2* This is why she loved him more. She had the same son as God, for he was born in her as man, and the All Highest himself established him. This is why she loved him the more incomparably. For she alone from eternity was worthy to have as son him who was also God.

Therefore, with deep calling to deep,* **Ps 42:7* two loves had come together into one and from the two loves was made a single love when the Virgin mother gave to her Son the love she gave to God and showed her love for her son in loving God. Therefore the more she loved, the more she grieved and the greatness of her love brought the increase of her suffering.

What was she doing when she stood on Calvary and saw the cross, the nails, the wounds of the One who was dying in innocency and the insatiable cruelty of the Pharisee afire with malice? He [Jesus] hung there atoning not for his sins but for ours, and the Pharisees with the Scribes, mocking him, struck him on the head and offered to his lips vinegar mingled

**Jn 19:29* with gall*—that there might be fulfilled the prophecy of David, saying in the person of Christ, 'They added **Ps 69:26* to the pain of my wounds.'* In the midst of this the Mother of God was distressed in mind and sorrows **Cf. Is 13:8* seized upon her as upon a woman in childbirth.* There are groans, sobs, sighs, sorrow, grief, agony, distress of heart, fires, a death more cruel than death. There life is not taken away yet the bitterness of death is suffered. O memory to be revered, full of devotion and tears, to recall how that glorious holy soul suffered, and what anguish she endured in the death of Christ. The pale face of Jesus reflected the bloodless face of his mother. He suffered in the flesh, she in her heart. Finally the insults and scoffing of the wicked came back upon his mother's head. The Lord's death was to her more bitter than her own [would have been]. Although, taught by the Spirit, she would not doubt the resurrection, yet she had to **Cf. Jn 18:11* drink the Father's cup* and to know the hour of her own passion. Concerning this, the venerable Simeon **Lk 2:35* prophesied to her: 'A sword shall pierce your soul.'* O Lord Jesus, terrible in your counsels beyond the **Ps 66:5* sons of men,* you did not spare your mother from **Ps 105:18* the sword piercing her soul.* By this road must we all pass by the fiery sword turning this way and that to **Gen 3:24* the tree of life which is in the midst of paradise.*

But to return: Blessed Mary was able to cry out that which was especially appropriate to Christ: 'O all you who pass by, behold and see if there is any **Lam 1:12* sorrow like my sorrow.'* What a sorrow and how great! And in that sorrow what was Mary like? Alas, as she was then, how different from the girl who had once tended her son amid a choir of angels while shepherds worshipped and Magi adored him with an offering of mystic gifts. Very different, not indeed in virtue but in sadness, not in grace but in grief. For she increased in virtue and grew in grace. For set in the midst of adversity she neither relaxed her modesty nor lost the strength of her constancy.

For proof of this, blessed Ambrose, bishop of Milan, says of her: 'I read of her standing by the Lord's cross, but I read not of her weeping.'* For to

*De obitu Valentiniani consolatio *39; PL 16: 1431D*

stand in such bitterness of heart is ascribable to her mighty constancy; to abstain from tears is the mark of the utmost self-control. She held back her tears from modesty, she stood there from a certain loftiness of soul. Therefore grief did not draw tears from her nor pain overthrow her spirit. For on the one side a befitting modesty, on the other a valiant constancy contended.

Therefore, beloved, let us imitate the Lord's mother so that in the midst of adversity we do not forget reserve and we remember constancy. Griefs will not be lacking, adversities will not be lacking, temptations will not be lacking, and death itself will make its way through us. Let us fortify our soul with humble reserve and firm constancy. Let our reserve continue in death and our constancy of spirit persist amid swords. Then being made by the likeness of our character like to the Mother of God, we shall be brought after her into the temple of the King,* **Ps 45:15* through the same Christ our Lord.

HOMILY VI

EAT, MY FRIENDS, drink and be inebriated, beloved.* I invite you to the table of wisdom and to libations of wine which she [wisdom] has mixed for you* in the bowl. I invite you to the banquet of the glorious lady, to the feast of the Mother of God. Happy he who, received at such a banquet, shall shine forth in the marriage garment amidst the guests.* The bread of life will be set before him, strengthening, filling, satisfying him with its wondrous sweetness, and the wine of gladness, the wine coming forth from the fruit of the vine, truly the wine of the resurrection pressed from the tree of the Lord's passion. This wine that grape produced which, brought from the promised land, hung upon the bar of wood.

*Sg 5:1

*Pr 9:5

*Cf. Mt 22:11

More, the aforesaid guest will eat, clad in a fine robe and wearing the ring of peace, after the fatted calf has been slain by the Father.* [He will eat] with his loins girt with the girdle of faith and chastity, having also shoes on his feet,* as being prepared for every good work,* and he will eat the flesh of the Paschal Lamb roasted with fire.* Nor will there be wanting, if the guest wishes, the fawn of a pleasant roe* and a stag leaping upon perfumed mountains, a leaping from the valley of hell to the mount of heaven.* Next, after taking the fish which was found near the sea shore above the plum trees,* when the Lord appeared to the disciples in the resurrection, he will at the same time taste the honey comb.* And taking the song of the Song of Songs, he will say on that day: 'I ate the comb with my honey. I drank my

*Cf. Lk 15:22

*Ex 12:11

*2 Tim 3:17

*Ex 12:8

*Cf. Pr 5:19

*Cf. Sg 2:8

*Cf. Jn 21:9-10

*Cf. Lk 24:42

*Sg 5:1
*Sg 8:5
*Sg 5:1

wine with my milk.'* Abounding then in every delight* he will invite others with him to the feast, saying, 'Eat, my friends, drink and be inebriated, beloved.'*

*Cf. Bernard, Dil XI, 32-3; CF 13; 123-5

I, too, brothers, invite you to this feast. Eat, drink, and be inebriated, beloved. Eat the bread of life, drink the wine of gladness, be inebriated with the joy of the resurrection. This inebriation is the height of sobriety.* It blots out remembrance of the world and always stamps upon the mind the thought of God's presence. Everyone drunk with this forgets all things and remembers only the charity of God. Therefore, be you also drunken, beloved, be drunken along with the Mother of God and rejoice. Rejoice in her joy, you who have mourned with her grief.

*Qo 3:4
*Mal 4:2
*Cf. Jn 10:9

Solomon says there is a time for joy and a time for grief.* Grief has departed, the time for joy has come, that true joy which proceeds from Christ's resurrection. For he has risen and he has raised up his mother's soul. She lay as in a narrow tomb of grief while the Lord lay in the sepulchre. As he arose, her spirit lived again and, waking as if from deep slumber, she saw in the morning light the sun of justice* and the rays of his rising. She gazed upon the beginning of the rising dawn and the future resurrection of her flesh, coming before time in her son. She feasted her eyes upon the glowing flesh of the risen Lord and in her heart perceived the glory of his godhead, so that within and without, leaving and entering, she enjoyed the pasturage of true and everlasting felicity.* Beside herself, therefore, forgetting self for joy, she clung with all her heart to the Father of spirits and bound fast to God she poured out upon him her whole self and was wholly flooded in the immensity of his love.

*Ps 21:1-3
*Source unknown

Lord, in your strength she rejoiced greatly and she will exult mightily in your saving help. You have granted her her heart's desire and not withheld from her the request of her life, since you have anticipated her with sweet blessings. You have placed on her head a crown of precious stone.* The crown of her head is Christ because, as the wise man says, a wise son is his mother's crown.* And who is wiser than he who is the Father's wisdom? It is rightly called a crown of stone because in the New Testament Christ is meant by the word 'stone'.* He was called stone because of his power, precious because of his glory. The psalmist, combining the two, says briefly, 'The Lord of hosts, he is the King of glory.'* Because he is Lord of hosts, he is therefore a stone. Because he is the king of glory, precious. Truly nothing is stronger than stone, nothing more precious than glory.

**Cf. Mt 21:42, Ps 118:22*

**Ps 24:10*

Therefore, O blessed one, you possess your joy. Your desire is fulfilled and Christ, your crown, has brought you through grace the sovereignty of heaven, through pity the kingdom of the world, through vengeance the submission of hell. For you the victor rose from hell, he wore down the gates of brass and broke the bars of iron.* He occupied hell's fortresses and crushed the dragon's head. He inflicted great slaughter upon his enemies and bound the prince of hell. He slew death and cast into chains the author of death. That author of death was bound with chains of fire.

**Ps 107:16*

Then he brought back his own from the darkness and broke their chains. He united with himself the souls of all the just, walking in the light of his countenance and rejoicing in his name.* Raised high by his justice are they who were brought low through injustice. The Lord Jesus was alone in his journey to hell, as David sang, saying for him: 'I am alone until I pass over.'* Alone as he entered but by no means alone as he went forth, for he brought back with him countless thousands of the saints. He fell to the earth and died that he might bear much fruit.* He laid himself down at seed time that he might at the harvest gather the human race.

**Ps 89:15-16*

**Ps 141:10*

**Cf. Jn 12:24-5*

Happy the womb of Mary in whom that seed took root. Happy she to whom it was said, 'your womb is like a heap of wheat set about with lilies.'* Was her womb not like a heap of wheat which swelled with that grain from which the whole harvest of the twice-born has grown? For at the baptismal font, dead to the sins within ourselves, we are born again

**Sg 7:2*

to Christ* through the cleansing of regeneration,* that we may live to him who died for all. So the Apostle says, 'as many of you as were baptized in Christ have put on Christ.'* Therefore from one grain come many harvests and that grain [came] from the virgin's womb. It is called a 'heap' from the power, not the number, of the seeds; from its strength, not its multiplicity.

*Cf. 2 Cor 5:15
*Tit 3:5
*Gal 3:27

It is said to be hedged about with lilies because the everlasting inviolability of the mother's womb is proved by the holy sayings of Scripture. What are the divine utterances but lilies diffusing the whiteness of purity and breathing a pleasing odor of sweetness? For this reason the Word and Wisdom of the Father is called the brightness of eternal light.* And concerning the holy utterances, the psalmist says: 'The words of the Lord are pure, silver tried in the fire, tested in the earth, seven times purified.'*

*Wis 7:26
*Ps 12:6

Concerning its perfume, it is written in the Canticle: 'We will run toward the perfume of your unguents.'* It is the voice of young maidens rejoicing in the fragrance of the bridegroom's words. 'We will run towards the perfume of your unguents', that is, to the knowledge of your utterances. For the utterances of the Lord are precious unguents, by which the sickness of souls is driven out and by which is applied the medicine appropriate to the wounds. By these antidotes the dread poisons of the serpent are scattered, to their warmth the cruel wounds yield, by their help is cured that wounded man who went down from Jerusalem to Jericho.* Again concerning their perfume, in the same Canticle, this is the voice of the Bridegroom to the bride: 'The fragrance of your unguents surpasses all perfumes.'* In another place he says, 'Your breasts are better than wine,* more fragrant than the best perfumes.'†

*Sg 1:3
*Cf. Lk 10:30ff
*Sg 4:10
*Ibid.
†Sg 1:2

The Church, the bride of Christ, has the breasts of the Testaments by which she pours the milk of consolation on her little ones, and on the full-grown the milk of exhortation.* It is no marvel the full-grown are nourished on her milk, for she says, 'I am a wall and my breasts are like a tower,

*Cf. William, Cant 40; CF 6:36-7, Bernard, SC 10:2; CF 4:62

therefore I have become in his presence as one seeking peace.'* *Sg 8:10

These breasts are said to be better than wine, for Paul bears witness: 'The foolishness of God is wiser than men.'* Better therefore are her breasts than the wine of empty philosophy, than the wine of earthly knowledge, than the wine of worldly greed, not indeed a wine pressed from the vineyard of Sorek* nor of Cyprus, nor the vineyard of Engedi,* but from the vineyard of Sodom and the outskirts of Gomorrha, or at least from the grapes of gall and the fruit of bitterness.*

*1 Cor 1:25

*Cf. Jg 16:5

*Sg 1:14

*Dt 32:32

Therefore young maidens, mindful of the bride's breasts, long to be nourished with an abundance of that milk rather than wine, that by it they may increase in health. 'Better are you breasts than wine fragrant with the choicest perfumes.'* *Sg 1:1-2

These breasts are fragrant with the choicest perfumes, since the aforesaid Testaments of the Church become known by their perfect utterances, so that in proportion to their ability to comprehend, some they feed with a veneer of history, others they teach by moral beauty, others they raise on high by their mystic meaning.* They are also fragrant with the choicest perfumes when to the same Testaments is added the grace of spiritual discernment and the virtue of divine charity, so that like certain lilies they shine white with the gift of discernment and are perfumed with the sweetness of love.

*On the levels of Scripture, see Cassian, Conf. 14,8 (forthcoming CS 20)

Among these lilies the beloved feeds, as the voice of his beloved says: 'My beloved,' she says, 'is mine and I am his, and he feeds among the lilies.'* He feeds among the lilies when the soul of the one who reads in the Scripture is satisfied with the inner sweetness of his word. Surrounded then by those lilies the Mother of God hears from the lips of Solomon, 'Your belly is as a heap of grain surrounded with lilies'.*

*Sg 2:16

*Sg 7:2

The souls of the saints can also be understood as lilies, gleaming white through the merit of their life, fragrant through their example. Of the whiteness the psalmist says to God: 'You shall purge me with hyssop and I shall be clean. You shall wash me and I

Ps 51:7 shall be whiter than snow.'* Concerning the perfume
Ps 45:1 he says: 'My heart has uttered a good word.'* The
Apostle also: 'We are the good perfume of Christ to
2 Cor 2:14-15 God in every place.'* Surrounded therefore by the
lilies of the redeemed, the Mother of the Redeemer
will most fittingly be able to say this word so appro-
Phil 4:1 priate to them: 'My joy and my crown.'* You have all
been gained by blood derived from my blood and by
flesh taken from my flesh.

With these lilies also was he hedged about when he
snatched the souls of the just from hell and blessed
them with the riches of his glory. The true Jacob
crossed the Jordan of mortality on the staff of the
Cf. Gen 32:10 cross and returned with two squadrons.* I understand
the two squadrons as circumcision and uncircumcision,
those who were under the Law and before the Law.
Therefore he died alone and lived again with great increase. For as in Adam all die, so in Christ shall all be
1 Cor 15:22 made alive.* By his death we have been increased, by
his blood our root has grown up, by his resurrection
our body has lived.

He has flowered not as grass but as the Word, not
as days of the world but as the days of heaven. Hence
by the voice of the Father it is said concerning the
seed of David: 'I will establish his seed for ever and his
Ps 89:29 throne as the days of heaven.'* Therefore an everlast-
Is 11:1 ing flower has sprung up from the root of Jesse;* it
was dried up by the passion but it flowered again at
the resurrection. It flowered again, not to wither
later like the flower of the field, but to remain the
Is 40:8 Word of God for ever.* For the Word was made flesh
Jn 1:14 and dwelt among us.* For that reason Daniel, a man
of longings, said that the Son of man came to the
ancient of days that he might show himself son of
Dn 9:23 man.* Seeing this the psalmist rightly says, 'Your
throne, O God, is for ever and ever. The sceptre of
righteousness is the sceptre of your kingdom. You
have loved righteousness and hated iniquity. Therefore God, your God, has anointed you with the oil of
Ps 45:6-7 gladness above your fellows.'* Look at him whom
God names, whose seat, he says, is for ever and ever.

After this he says that this one was anointed by

God with the oil of gladness above his fellows. For being God from eternity, he reigns with the Father for ever, and as man in time is anointed with the oil of gladness above his fellows. He was truly above his fellows, for the Father says to him: 'You are my son. This day have I begotten you.'* And that saying: 'Sit on my right hand until I make your enemies your footstool.'* That you may know that he is equal to the Father as touching his divinity, hear him say in the Gospel: 'I and the Father are one',* and 'He who sees me sees also the Father.'*

**Ps 2:7* **Ps 110:1* **Jn 10:30* **Jn 14:9*

Of him also the Apostle says: 'Therefore God has exalted him and given him a name above every name, that at the name of Jesus, every knee should bow, of things in heaven, things on earth, and of things under the earth.'* In truth, the knee of those in hell bends before him in dread, the knee of those on earth through self-interest, of those in heaven through their blessedness. On the first he inflicts punishment, the second he brings out from their wretchedness, the third he raises in glory. To the first he is terrible in judgement, to the second pitiful in aiding them, to the third generous in rewarding them. He subdues the demons with his sword, redeeming men with his blood, satisfying the angels with the sight of his countenance. Therefore hell bends the knee, trembling at his power; earth bows the knee, praising his mercy. Heaven bends the knee crying out 'Holy, Lord God of hosts. Heaven and earth are full of his glory.'*

**Ph 2:9-10* **Is 6:3*

He himself is your son, O Mary, he himself rose from the dead on the third day and with your flesh ascended above all the heavens that he might fill all things. Therefore, O blessed lady, you have your joy, the object of your desire and the crown of your head have been granted you. He has brought to you the sovereignty of heaven through his glory, the kingdom of the world through his mercy, the subjugation of hell through his power. All things with their diverse feelings respond to your great and unspeakable glory: angels by honor, men by love, demons by terror. For you are venerated in heaven, loved in the world, feared in hell.

Rejoice therefore and be glad, for he who receives you has arisen, your glory, lifting up your head.* You rejoiced at his conception, you were afflicted at his passion. Rejoice again in his resurrection and your joy no one will take from you.* Christ, rising from the dead, dies no more. Death will have no more dominion over him.* The spirit calls you, God says to you: 'Arise, hasten, my love, my dove, my fair one and come. For the winter is past, the rain has departed and gone, the flowers have appeared on our earth. The time for pruning has come.'*

**Ps 3:3*
**Jn 16:22*
**Rom 6:9*
**Sg 2:10-12*

My love by wedlock, my dove by union, my fair one through your beauty and elegance. Rise up from grief, from affliction, from humiliation and out of the dust, which are the marks of sorrow. Hasten, away with delay, shake off your burden, put off your heaviness, put on lightness, run, take wing, and come. Come that you who lately grieved may rejoice, come that you may see the glory of God, the first fruits of the resurrection, the first born from the dead.* Now the winter is past in which Peter, benumbed, denied, in which the frozen hearts of the Jews extinguished for themselves the sun of justice,* having kindled the embers of their passions. The rain is over and gone, the stormy downpour, bringing mud, bringing ruin, mingled with snow and hail, it is over and gone. The rain of those who cried out and said: 'Crucify, crucify him'* is over and gone. Gone too the rain by which the Gentiles' threshing floor was deemed worthy to be watered, while the fleece of the Jewish people was dried up.*

**Cf. Col 1:18*
**Cf. Mal 4:2*
**Jn 19:6*
**Cf. Jg 6:40*

Flowers have appeared in our land, flowers everywhere of blessed spirits and of angels blooming in alternation and sprinkling the place where the Lord has been laid with sweet perfume. These the Old Testament set forth in symbol when above the mercy seat at either end it set up two carven cherubim or painted them with palms on the doors of the tabernacle.* The meaning is clear: hidden then in symbols, now revealed in reality. Palms bear the sign of the resurrection. The doors and the mercy seat point to him who is the open door to the kingdom

**Cf. Ex 37:7-9, 1 K 6:29*

and the propitiation for the sins of men.* The two cherubim are the two angels who sat one at the head and one at the feet where the body of Christ had been laid.*

*1 Jn 2:2

*Jn 20:12

They are rightly called flowers because the eternity of the high God gives them an eternal spring so that they always bloom, never wither, never fall, and remain the same with their beauty untouched. Flowers also appeared in our land when, as the Lord ascended, two men stood by the apostles, and said to them, 'Men of Galilee, why do you marvel as you gaze into heaven? This Jesus who has been taken from you will come, just as you have seen him go into heaven.'*

*Ac 1:11

The time for pruning has come. Hell has been pruned and the devil has been cut off from the heart of the believer. The mouth of the Lord has separated the precious from the worthless,* cutting the dead twigs from the vines and gathering the darnel from out of the harvest, that he may heap the grain into the barns, throwing the weeds on the pyre to be burnt.*

*Jer 15:19

*Cf. Mt 13:30

O unhappy separation! Grief and joy everywhere intermingled. O sweet and bitter day, when the righteous judge, returning from hell, on some turned his back, to others showed the face they longed for. Some he abandoned for punishment, others he raised as joint heirs in his kingdom. The former he sent away to burn with the devil,* the latter he carried with him to be crowned in heaven. The wicked saw it and groaned in hopelessness. The good saw it and rejoiced with all their heart.

*Cf. Mt 25:41

O wretched ones whom mercy did not aid! O blessed ones, to whom it came in glory. O wicked ones whom even the passion of the Only-begotten did not help. O happy ones, whom it rescued from eternal death. The wicked saw and groaned in hopelessness. The good saw and together lifted up their voice in triumph.

And you, glorious lady, saw your Son rising from hell. You saw with your blessed eyes your son's glory. You saw and you fainted. Your flesh and your

Ps 73:26 heart failed.* You turned to water when you heard
Sg 5:6 the voice of your beloved* son speaking to you. His
word became like a fire burning in your bones. Therefore inflamed by the divine words you became wholly like a fire and you offered yourself as a sweet sacrifice to God. O phoenix, sending forth perfume more
Cf. Si 24:20 pleasing than cinnamon and balsam,* sweeter than
nard delighting the king by its presence. O phoenix, gathering together all chosen beauties, surrounded by supersubstantial fire, that you may fill the heaven of heavens and the angelic powers of heaven with a wondrous sweet incense. This incense is most sweet, this well-compounded frankincense comes forth from the censer of Mary's heart and sweetly surpasses
Cf. Ex 30:34-8 every perfume.*

Then the censer following the incense and lifted up by the hand of the Lord mounts to the throne of God. It goes up attended by a train of angelic spirits calling out on high and saying, 'who is this who comes up through the desert like a column of smoke from the odor of myrrh and incense and all the powders
Sg 3:6 of the perfume?'*

But now let our discourse [now] brought as far as the ascension be brought to an end, so that with God's help another may more fully describe this ascension. Amen.

HOMILY VII

AS I REFLECT and often ponder over in my mind the assumption of the Mother of God, a certain question comes to my mind, worthy of examination, profitable when answered, which will obviously be pleasant when it is shared. The question is why, when the Lord ascended into heaven, did his mother who embraced him with such affection not follow him at once? Since she was weighed down with no cloud of sin, soiled with no spot on her life, glowed more than a fire because of her charity, was brighter than the light by reason of her chastity, even outdistanced the denizens of heaven through the uniqueness of the virgin birth, it seemed strange that she was not carried at once to heaven with her Son.

Doubtless Enoch walked with God in purity of heart and was seen no more, for God took him.* *Gen 5:24 Elijah also, burning with the great fire of charity, is said to have been carried away by a chariot of fire and horses of fire.* *2 K 2:11 But she who surpassed Enoch in purity of heart and was greater than Elijah through the privilege of her love, why was she not straightway carried into heaven along with him whom she bore? For she was full of grace and blessed among women.* *Lk 1:28 She alone was found worthy to conceive true God from true God.* *Cf. Nicene Creed She, a virgin, bore him. She, a virgin, gave him suck, cherishing him in her arms, in all ways she served him with the reverence of an underling. Finally she suffered with him in his death, more in mind than in body. She lived again in the Spirit in his resurrection, and why did she not ascend with him in his ascension? Her sacred flesh

which was pregnant by the Holy Spirit, which
swelled by the seed of the mighty King, in which God
Jn 1:14 was made man and the Word became flesh, and by
the mediation of Christ the fulness of his divinity
Col 2:9 remained in her bodily, [that flesh] would seem
meet to be brought to heaven when the Lord was
taken up. Why was she held back even for a moment?
Why did she suffer separation from her Son? Why was
her holy desire, hotter than fire, held back?

Because that delay was no small comfort for
Christ's disciples. That delay did not detract from the
mother and it brought to the world the medicines of
salvation. For the Lord Jesus willed that on his
return to his Father his disciples should enjoy
maternal comfort and teaching. Though indeed they
had been taught by the Spirit, yet they could be
taught by her who put forth to the world the sun of
Cf. Mal 4:2 righteousness and brought for us from a virgin
meadow, from an unspotted womb, the fount of
Cf. Si 1:5 wisdom. In short, with wondrous goodness provi-
sion was made for the primitive Church which no
longer saw God present in the flesh, that it might see
his mother and be refreshed by the lovely sight.

For what is there so lovely, so seemly and delightful, as to behold the mother of the Creator and
Redeemer of the world? If the sepulchre of that same
Redeemer, which still exists today, is so delightful in
our sight, if the stone on which rested the holy stock
Cf. Is 11:1 of Jesse is sought out by such a great concourse that
it calls forth the affections and thoughts of all men
and attracts everything by a kind of religious charm,
what joy was it to see the Mother of God as long as
the divine pity allowed her to stay with us on earth in
our common life?

Ps 33:12 Blessed nation and happy generation which was
worthy to be enlightened with such a sight. Blessed
indeed the generation in whose midst, believing and
rejoicing, stood the tree producing the life-giving
Cf. Gen 3:3,22 fruit. The mother of the true light shone forth, and
there was seen that well, closed and sealed, from
which issued the spring of the house of David, open
Zec 13:1 for the washing away of sin and defilement. This

unique privilege, this heavenly gift, this special grace was offered to the primitive Church.

Finally the virgin Mother granted a share in all the gifts of grace within her. For as soon as she was seen glowing with the fire of holy love, she sweetly inflamed the hearts of those near her, brought faith to the hearts, urged them to modesty, made what was honorable lovely, drawing them to righteousness. She breathed the flower of virginity, sowed the untilled field of chastity, portraying before their eyes the picture of humility and showing them the mark of truthfulness. Around her was an unfailing brightness and in her face a glowing fire.* A swift-flowing river of fire went forth from her* to set on fire her foes, to warm her friends, to help her neighbors, to burn up her enemies. It is said by those who understand the nature of living things that the poisonous snake by the mere sight of it and by its deadly breath kills whatever is near it. In the same way she, hotly inflamed by its nearness with the heat of the divine fire and sprinkled with the blazing flames of the Word, breathed forth the scent of the grace of the resurrection upon those who were far off and those who were near.*

**Cf. Ps 18:8*
**Dan 7:10*
**Is 57:19*

Indeed for some, that is those against her, it was the odor of death into death, but for others who believed in her Son the odor of life into life.* For as in Eve all die, so in Mary will all be made alive.* And as by the sin of Eve comes the condemnation of the world, so by Mary's faith has come to pass the world's restoration. The one [Eve] was infected with a deadly poison which she handed on to her posterity. The other [Mary] was filled with a life-giving antidote which she transmitted to all the faithful. The one fell, mistakenly trusting the serpent; the other rose up and, according to the word which in Genesis God had before spoken, bruised the serpent's head,* having been foretold from the beginning and now presented to the primitive Church, once promised and now revealed at the end of the age.

**Cf. 2 Cor 2:16*
**Cf. 1 Cor 15:22*
**Gen 3:15*

Who would not hasten, who would not run from the ends of the earth to gaze upon the beauty of the venerable majesty and to behold the countenance endowed with all manner of sweetness and with commanding dignity and unique power? Indeed, nothing was found like to her among the sons and daughters of Adam, none such among the prophets, apostles or angels. Heaven and earth have put forth nothing like her. Who in the clouds would equal her* or be like the Mother of the Lord among the sons of God?

**Cf. Ps 89:6*

And see how fittingly before her assumption her wonderful name blazed forth in the whole world and her renown was everywhere spread abroad before her grandeur was raised above the heavens.* For it was fitting that the Virgin Mother, for the honor of her Son, should reign first upon earth and then, at last, receive the heavens with glory, should tarry in the depths that she might enter the heights in the fulness of sanctity; and just as she was carried from virtue to virtue so by the Spirit of the Lord be borne from esteem to esteem.*

**Cf. Ps 8:1*

**2 Cor 3:18*

Therefore while present in the flesh she tasted in advance the first-fruits of the future kingdom, now going forth to God in unspeakable sublimity, now in wondrous charity condescending to her neighbors. On the one side she was attended by the services of angels, on the other venerated by the devotion of man. Gabriel, the groomsman, with the angels was at her side; John, with the apostles, ministered to her, rejoicing that at the cross the Virgin Mother was entrusted to him.* These [the angels] rejoiced to see their queen; those [the apostles] to see their lady, and all obeyed her with pious devotion.

**Jn 19:27*

But she, dwelling in the lofty citadel of the virtues and enriched by an ocean of divine gifts, poured out in generous diffusion upon a believing and thirsting people an abyss of graces, in which she surpassed all others. She brought health to their bodies and cure to their souls, being powerful to raise them from the death of body and soul. Who ever went away from her sick or sad and not knowing heavenly mysteries? Who did not return to his home glad and joyful, having obtained from the Mother of God his wish?

The presence of Mary brought the sweet warmth of spring, and wherever she turned with her favor was paradise. 'Your plants,' said the Spouse, 'are an orchard of pomegranates and apples: cypress oil with nard, nard and saffron, calamus and cinnamon, with all the trees of Lebanon, myrrh and aloes, with all the chief spices, a fountain for gardens, a well of living waters and swift streams from Lebanon.'* For the garden of the glorious lady has pomegranates in the variety of her virtues, pleasant fruits in the perfection of her works. She has also cypress-oil with nard, the one heavy with grapes, the other a fragrant herb with wondrous odor, because of the sober intoxication of her senses and the sweet and fragrant esteem of her virtues. To these are added the saffron of gladness, the calamus of the ravaging of the flesh, the cinnamon of sweet gentleness, with all the trees of Lebanon by which is typified the sum total of all her virtues. The myrrh of mortification and the aloes of incorruption, with all the chief perfumes, poured out without loss of that perfume which poured upon the head and came down to the beard, Aaron's beard;* not the Aaron of old, who was the type, but the new one, the typified. And it came down to the hem of his garment,* which is the Church, presented—as Paul says—to that true Aaron without spot of wrinkle.* The bride therefore, enriched with these great gifts, mother of only bridegroom, sweet and beloved for her charms, as a spring in spiritual gardens and as a well of living and life-giving waters which flow swiftly from the divine Lebanon,* distributed from Mount Sion to all the peoples round about rivers of peace and the overflowings of grace poured out from heaven.*

*Sg 4:13-15

*Ps 133:2

*Ibid.

*Eph 5:27

*Sg 4:15

*Cf. Is 66:12

Blessed David, speaking of his son our Lord, says: 'There will be in his day righteousness and abundance of peace'; then presently speaking of her he rightly added: 'until the moon be taken away'.* She is indeed the moon which lighting up the heavens and the earth shines far brighter than the stars (that is, the saints), 'until,' he says, 'the moon be taken away'; the moon which when the sun of righteousness arose

*Ps 72:7

stayed in its own place and first shone forth upon the primitive Church.

The faith of our ancestors according to true history relates that from the birth of the Saviour to the passing of the glorious lady the world's inhabitants rested in calm unbroken peace, the madness of war being stilled. These things we have said in answer to the question set before us, that we might show with what advantage the death of the mother of our King was postponed.

Indeed, we must mark also how from this postponement every faithful soul, wounded with charity, pierced with the darts of love, learns not to complain that it does not go hence in answer to its prayers. Look, the Mother of the Lord suffers delay, who would dare to murmur? She suffers delay that she may advance, she advances through her perseverance. Perseverance, joined to love and work, creates fulness, brings forth perfection. Hence comes what is rightly spoken by the voice of the psalmist: 'the righteous will flower as the palm tree, as the cedar of

**Ps 92:12*

Lebanon will he be multiplied.'* The palm is said to flower after a long space of time and the cedar of Lebanon multiplies after a long passage of years. So the righteous, as his soul grows white with age, will flower like the palm with the long lapse of time. The said psalmist aptly added a few words: 'They will still

**Ps 92:14*

be multiplying in ripe old age.'* We should then note that Mary, endowed with surpassing merit and unique righteousness, who was worthy to be exalted above the angels, had first to be multiplied here in a fruitful old age. When this came to pass by God's gift, her hidden being and the beauty which she wore in secret (having become brighter than light and surpassing every loveliness) turned towards her the faces and hearts of the citizens above with wondrous love.

But now, who would worthily extol her holy assumption? Who unfold in words how joyfully she went forth from the body, how joyfully she beheld her Son, how exultingly she hastened to the Lord, attended by choirs of angels, supported by the reverence of apostles, while she beheld the King in his beauty* and saw her Son awaiting her with glory, free from every ill as she was free from all corruption? She was brought forth from the house of her flesh to live for ever with Christ. She passed over in the vision of God, she breathed out to God her blessed soul, brighter than the sun, higher than the heavens, of more worth than the angels. For by her glorious passing is lit up Mount Sion, where at the end of her days she passed away in happy old age. It was there that she completed the last service of her life, giving full and perfect fulfilment of all her virtues. There the armies of God hasten to meet her rising not dying, departing not dying, and the heavenly hosts hasten to meet her.

*Is 33:17

How precious in the sight of God is his mother's death!* What life will equal her death? What joy her passing? You may bring together earthly loves, feasts and triumphal banquets, everything that sweetens and delights the whole world, yet this [death] is lovelier and sweeter than them all. For it is a liberation from the flesh, a road to life involving no pain, no bitterness, no terror. In place of pain, it cherishes; instead of bitterness it delights; and in place of terror it strengthens the faith of the one who stands on the shore. It brings no darkness, for it reveals eternal light. It does not take away life for it directs to the author of life.

*Cf. Ps 116:15

By this death the glorious lady departed, if we may call a passing into life 'death'. Rather, to speak truly, life is where death alone dies, where the body of death is shed, where the life of the flesh now departed in a holy rest is preserved for the time to come with manifest gains. Is it not life when one goes to the source of life and drinks eternal life from life in an unbroken stream? Of this unfailing draught the virgin Mother tasted even before her death, so that in her very passing she should not be touched by the slightest taste of death. Therefore as she went forth she saw life, that she might not see death. She saw her Son that she might not grieve at her separation from the flesh. Therefore going out free with such a happy vision and being possessed of the face of God that she had longed for, she found the revered citizens of heaven ready to render service and attend her.

They marvel that this soul of unique merit, freed from the everlasting taint of sin had not a spot of the flesh or of the world. They marvel that, freed from the body, she glowed with the grace of perfect purity. What should they first praise in her: integrity or humility, prudence or charity, vigor of mind or forbearance, the honor of her motherhood or the novelty of the birth? But yet more praised in her is her perfect virtue and fulness of grace.

Therefore the Lord, present at her departure from the body, thus proclaims her prasies: '*You are all lovely,* my mother, *and there is no spot in you.*
*Sg 4:7 *You are all lovely, he says,** lovely in thought, lovely in word, lovely in deed, lovely from your beginning to your end, lovely in the virgin conception, lovely in the divine birth, lovely in the crimson of my passion, lovely in the brightness of my glorious resurrection. *Arise, therefore, my beloved, my dove, my fair one,* my spotless one, *and come, for the winter* of my absence *is past, the rain* of your tears *has departed and gone* and with the sun's return, angelic *flowers appear* for you. Your *voice,* chaste dove, *has been heard. The time* of your
*Sg 2:10-12 assumption *has come.*'*

Therefore when the Virgin of virgins was led by God and his Son, the King of kings, amid angels triumphant, archangels rejoicing and heaven resounding with praises, there was fulfilled the prophecy of David saying to the Lord: 'The queen stood on your right hand in vesture of gold wrought about with
Ps 45:9 divers colors.' Then according to the word of Solomon: 'Daughters have risen up and called her
Cf. Pr 31:28 blessed and queens alike have praised her.' 'Who is she,' says the heavenly virtues, 'who ascends in white,
Cf. Sg 8:5 leaning upon her beloved?' And again: 'Who is she who goes forth like the rising dawn, fair as the moon,
Cf. Sg 6:9 choice as the sun?' Again they said: 'Who is she who goes up through the desert like a column of smoke from perfumes of myrrh and incense and all the
Sg 3:6 powders of the perfumers?' That splendor is for us

strange and wondrous, strange and glorious, this plan of her assumption, strange and pleasing this most sweet odor.

Escorted amid such praises, she herself could not refrain from praising, for she saw the Son of God, born of her, sitting on the right hand of his Father's majesty, receiving her with glory. 'You have held,' she says, 'my right hand, and have led me according to your will and received me with glory'.* And again: 'He is at my right hand lest I be moved. Therefore my heart has rejoiced and my tongue has exulted. Still more my flesh shall rest in hope. Since you did not abandon me in the world nor did you give your Mother's body to see corruption.'*

Ps 73:23-4

Cf. Ps 16:8-10

But why do I linger over these things? To sum up much in a few words: there was with the most glorious lady a word simple yet complex, a word understandable, containing all the words of praise with which she herself honored the Lord and Son with praise unutterable.

Exalted therefore with cries of exultation and praise, she is placed in her seat of glory first after God, above all the company of heaven. There, having taken again the substance of her flesh (for it is not lawful to believe that her body saw corruption) and clothed with a double robe,* she looks upon God and man in his two natures with a gaze clearer than all others, inasmuch as it is more burning than all, with the eyes of her soul and body.

Cf. Pr 31:21

Then coming down to the human race in ineffable charity and turning upon us those eyes of pity* with which heaven is brightened, she lifts her prayer alike for clergy, for the people of either sex, for the living and for the departed. Here from heaven is the glorious Virgin most powerful in prayer, driving away every hurtful thing and bestowing what is good, and she grants to all who pray to her from the heart her protection for this present life and for that to come.

Cf. Salve Regina *hymn*

For remembering for what purpose she was made the Mother of the Redeemer, most willingly she gathers up the sinner's prayers and pleads with her Son for all the guilt of those who are penitent. Surely she will gain what she wishes, the dear Mother through whose chaste womb the Word of God came to us, the sin offering of the world, to wash away with his own blood the bond of original sin, Jesus Christ Our Lord, who lives and reigns with God the Father in the unity of the Holy Spirit, God for ever and ever. Amen.

HOMILY VIII

SEVERAL DAYS, beloved, have passed in which, under the burden of the episcopate and encumbered with great anxieties, I have been unable to provide for your holy hunger the promised meal concerning the praise of blessed Mary. Now therefore, if the blessed Virgin favors me, I will not fail you, withdrawing myself indeed a little from my affairs but inclining to your pious wishes.

Therefore let us with unremitting duty do honor to the Queen of Heaven, Mother of Life, Fount of Pity, abounding in charm and resting upon her Beloved,* **Cf. Sg 8:5*
and let us laud her—though our praise be inadequate. Let us in spirit be raised on high, noting carefully that the beauteous rod sprang from the root of Jesse* by **Is 11:1*
the marvellous spreading of its branches stretched over the whole world,* that with welcome shade it **Cf. Ps 80:11*
might protect the scattered sons of Adam from heat, from tempest and from rain, and nourish the hungry with health-giving fruit. Towering therefore over all the trees of paradise and raised above the lofty summits of the highest mountains, she, in her unbelievable greatness, entered heaven itself, attended by the choirs of the heavenly orders and honored by the dances of virgins.

O the splendor, glory and magnificence of this tree by whose never-failing fruit, by whose undying nourishment there is provided a perpetual feast for the inhabitants of heaven and earth, an unbroken rejoicing, a blissful and never-ending praise. Blessed are they who eat meat in your kingdom.* Blessed are **Cf. Lk 14:15*
they who dwell, O Lord, in your house. For ever

**Ps 84:4*
**Gen 3:20*

and ever will they praise you.* In you also shall be praised not Eve, who gave death to drink, but Mary, giver of life, mother and nurse of all men, life of the living.* In you shall your mother be praised.

**Ps 34:2*
**Cf. Is 14:12*
**Cf. Ps 66:33*
**Ps 41:8*
**Cf. Ps 62:2*

Let the gentle hear and rejoice.* Lucifer the boastful has been wounded and falls to the depths.* Let the proud hear and be brought low. The humble virgin is crowned and mounts to the throne of glory. Let the humble hear and be glad. He has fallen, he that was raised on high by his great presumption. Mary has entered among the burnt offerings* by yielding herself wholly to the fulness of grace. He, hardened with ill will, will never proceed to rise again.* She, strengthened by charity, will never be so shaken as to fall.* For clinging with unshakeable firmness to the immovable centre, she could never be disturbed by any changeableness. He, going beyond the noble bounds of angelic dignity, striving after that which a created spirit does not approach, pursuing a mere void, rushes over steep places, is shrouded in a dark horror, sliding down to the depths of the pit to grieve eternally and to pay the penalty in the torments of a just damnation.

**Isidore of Seville,* Etymologiarum *8. 11. 18; PL 82:316A*
**Ps 75:5*
**Cf. Mt 23:7*

He who is rightly named the devil, that is, 'falling backwards'* (because he disappeared from the heights, envying those who stood firm), he plunged with himself into the depths those whom he could. He prompted those who trusted him to seek for honors, position, superiority, to savor what is lofty, to lift their horn on high,* to love the applause of the crowd, greetings in the marketplace, the first seats at gatherings,* to scorn their inferiors, to put themselves before their equals, to envy their betters, to forget the glory of God, to bring under their sway some by flattery, others by threats or torture, to set themselves up as idols, to do all things to be seen of men and to be praised.

When he has raised to the clouds these wretched ones, proud, puffed up, amazed and demented, then finally he turns the same ones, cruelly enfeebled, towards all that is shameful and dishonorable; and when they are so turned he hurls them, along with himself, without pity into the depths of hell.

But the glorious Virgin, with flesh untouched and tranquil mind, gentlest of the living, the lowlier and holier she is than all others, the higher was she raised above all and she was received into heaven by its citizens with every mark of honor and in the fashion of a queen and was bidden by the Supreme Father to sit down in the kingdom of eternal brightness and on the throne of surpassing glory, first in rank after the Son whom she bore incarnate.

Mighty God, terrible and strong,* of unspeakable goodness, you raise and exalt your humble handmaid to the place from which you had long ago driven out your jealous foe, so that humility might triumph, adorned by you with the increase of grace and a glorious crown,* yet pride, empty and dark, might fall in ruin.

Cf. Neh 1:5

Pr 4:9

Conspicuous therefore by her unparalleled merit the blessed lady stands before the face of her Creator interceding always for us with her powerful prayer.* Taught by that light to which all things are bare and open,* she sees all our dangers, and our merciful and sweet lady pities us with motherly affection.

Cf. Heb 7:25

Heb 4:13

The holy creatures of which one reads in Ezekiel that they are full of eyes before and behind, within and without and round about,* cannot weigh as can the Mother of God the toils of men, their griefs, misfortunes, failures, blindness, weaknesses, deadly perils, the uncertain end of life and every ill of the human race and, by weighing them, with heaven's help dispense and drive them away. The more she beholds from on high the heart of the mighty king the more profoundly she knows, by the grace of divine pity, how to pity the unhappy and to help the afflicted.

Ezk 1:18

So she was called Mary, that is, star of the sea, in the foreseeing purpose of God, that she might declare by her name that which she manifests more clearly in reality.* For from the time she ascended to the heavens to reign with her Son, robed in beauty, robed equally in strength, she has girded herself, ready to curb with a single gesture the extraordinary

Cf. Bernard, Miss II.17

Ps 92:1,4 tumults of the sea.* For those who sail upon the sea of the present age and call upon her with complete faith she rescues from the breath of the storm and the raging of the winds and brings them, rejoicing with her, to the shore of their happy country. One cannot tell, beloved, how often some would have struck hard rocks, about to suffer shipwreck, some fall on foul sandbanks to return no more, some the whirlpool
See Aeneid *III. 432, 684, V. 122* Scylla would have engulfed in its fearsome depth,* some the Siren's sweet songs would detain to their
*Ibid. *V. 864* destruction,* did not the star of the sea, Mary ever virgin, stand in the way with her mighty aid and when now the rudder was broken, the deck shattered, and they were without human aid, bring them by her heavenly leading to the haven of inner peace.

Therefore rejoicing in new triumphs in the new rescue of the boat, in the new additions of peoples, she manifests her joy in the Lord and, not content with spoils she has won but eager for man's salvation, the malicious foe driven further and further away, she is always winning more and more trophies. So with
Ps 136:12 powerful hand and arm upraised* she advances into the tyrant's realms, attacks all the strongholds of the demons, making hell tremble beneath her feet and the prince of death shrink back, struck with a mighty dis-
Jb 40:10 may. Finally, at her bidding Behemoth* spews forth the prey which he had made to pass into his malicious belly, casting out with regret that which he held in his inordinate arrogance. The fallen arise, the penitent
Ps 112:10 return. The sinner will see and will rage.* His jaw,
See above, Hom V, p. 101 pierced with the hook of the Saviour's cross,* gives back as freedom those whom before he held captive,
Ps 112:10 gnashing his teeth and wasting away.* Through the Mother they are reconciled to the Son, through the Virgin they are reconciled to God, being given back to life, utterly withdrawn from death.

The desire of sinners will perish, but the desire of blessed Mary is fulfilled when every day those in chains are led forth from the pit of sorrow and its
Ps 40:2 muddy dregs,* so that from the prison-house of sin and the depths of iniquity they may breathe, by the gift of pardon, the air of everlasting freedom. Thus

she gathers together those who were scattered, she calls back the wanderers, rescuing those being led to death. And those whom she sees being dragged to torment she ceases not to set at liberty. Not only for the salvation of their souls but also for the health of men's bodies she takes thought and heals them, and with duteous care takes thought for their needs. In the places dedicated to her holy memory she wins movement for the lame, sight for the blind, hearing for the deaf, speech for the dumb,* curing every kind of weakness and affording countless gifts of healing. **Cf. Mt 11:5*

There come to her doors men beating their breasts, confessing their sins, and having received pardon they return home with joy. There come also those who are sick in mind, weak in the head, the mad, the maniacs, the possessed, those who are led astray by nightly terrors, by some phantasma or by a genuine attack of the evil one, and they regain their health and receive the generosity of the divine gift. In the same way there draw near to her feet those whose hearts are bitter: the sad, the needy, the afflicted, the lonely, those tied up by debt and, most grievous of all, those living in dishonor and besmirched with the stain of ill-repute.

The prayers of all these who cry out of whatever tribulation she gladly receives and, making supplication to her Son, in her pity she turns from them every evil. For just as wax melts at the touch of fire and as ice melts in the heat of the sun, so the army of her foes perishes before her face and at her bidding nothing hostile stands.

But we must mark and carefully consider with what love, with what great kindness she embraces and loves those who are akin to her in purity of heart, she who, as has often been said, by her intercession constantly frees from the death of sin and from eternal pains worthless and wicked men. Indeed, glowing and conspicuous with this twofold love on the one hand, she is most ardently fixed upon God to whom she clings and she is one spirit with him;* on the other she gently comforts and attracts the hearts of the elect and shares with them excellent gifts **Cf. 1 Cor 6:17*

coming from the generosity of her Son. Therefore with her swift motion outstripping the winged
**Cf. Is 6:2* seraphim,* now at the fount of life she enjoys the love of the Godhead, now lighting up the world with her miracles and powers she everywhere succours her own as a joyful, openhanded mother.

Some men her presence makes conquerors by subduing their vices, some by her kindly intercession she makes possessors of great virtues; to certain ones she reveals the secret of interior contemplation, to others at their end she shows the sure road, so that no might of the enemy dismays those whom the Mother of the Only-begotten God guides to Christ.

There are very many examples of what has been said which we shall for the sake of brevity omit as being generally well-known. But you must know for certain that frequent miracles, countless benefits, spiritual visions, heavenly revelations, lofty consolations of the gentle Mother of the Lord will constantly shine forth in the world until the world itself grows old and finds its end, as dawns the Kingdom of
**Lk 1:33* which there is no end.*

But meanwhile there comes to mind that notable day of judgement whose greatness the holy prophet
**Cf. Ps 56:4* David declared he fears,* and which all the faithful always know to be approaching. In that moment of awful examination the King of heaven will be present with his holy mother, attended by angels and archangels and the whole army of the heavenly host to judge the world in righteousness and its inhabitants
**Ps 98:9* with justice.*

Then will she shine forth in glorious light, she through whose virgin womb and closed door God the king of glory shone upon the world. Then will be revealed the truth of patriarchs and prophets who witnessed aforetime to the god-bringing childbearing of the Virgin. Her Son's apostles, imitators and witnesses of her virtues, will also bring to her glory and honor, for illuminated by his teaching and strengthened by the spirit of wisdom that fell upon them from heaven, they have filled the Church with the splendor of the true sun.

Martyrs will rejoice, seeing the glorious lady whom on earth they loved, whose merits while life lasted they celebrated with their praise. They will rejoice, I say, gazing on that unique diadem which on that day of solemnity and joy, the day of her assumption and glory, Christ placed upon the head of his beloved mother, calling to mind the crown with which she had crowned him on the day of the betrothal.* **Sg 3:11*

Virgins will run in the scent of her perfumes,* **Sg 1:3* hastening to enter with her into the wedding that, joined with her for ever in the heavenly marriage chamber to their true spouse, they may sing, with Mary leading the new song* which no one can utter **Rev 14:3* unless he be virgin in spirit and body. Lastly each sex, every age, every rank and every honor will call her most blessed and a people beyond counting will cry out to her in jubilation, being saved by her merits and prayers and crowned at his right hand by the good Lord.

May it be our good fortune to be in their number and in their fellowship, o tender, o sweet Mary, so that when the day of wrath comes, the day of tribulation and of grief,* we may not be punished for our **Zeph 1:15* sin, but through you, Lady, we may be deemed worthy of his mercy who ascended to the Father to prepare a place* for his servants that he might set **Jn 14:2* them in the lovely country of heaven, in the bright resting places of paradise, amid the sparkling fiery stones of Jesus Christ our Lord, whose is the splendor, honor, power, glory and greatness
with the same Father and the Holy
Spirit, through infinite
ages of ages.
Amen.

ABBREVIATIONS

ASOC	*Analecta Sacri Ordinis Cisterciensis / Analecta Cisterciensis.* Rome, 1945–
Bern	The Works of Bernard of Clairvaux
Dil	*Liber de diligendo deo (On Loving God)*
Miss	*Homilia super missus est in laudibus Virginis Matris (Homilies in Praise of the Virgin Mother)*
SC	*Sermo super Cantica canticorum (Sermons on the Song of Songs)*
CF	Cistercian Fathers Series. Cistercian Publications
Conf.	The Conferences of John Cassian
CS	Cistercian Studies Series. Cistercian Publications
Hom	Homily
PL	J. P. Migne, *Patrologiae cursus completus, series latina.* 221 volumes. Paris, 1844–64.
SBOp	*Sancti Bernardi Opera,* edd. J. Leclercq, H. M. Rochais, C. H. Talbot. Rome, 1957–
William	The Works of William of Saint Thierry
Cant	*Expositio super Cantica canticorum* (Exposition on the Song of Songs)

Scriptural quotations have been translated directly from the Latin and cited according to the enumeration and nomenclature of the Jerusalem Bible.

INDEX

(Arabic numerals refer to pages)

INDEX OF PERSONS